Rain Gardening in the South

Rain Gardening in the South

Ecologically Designed Gardens for
Drought, Deluge, and Everything in Between

HELEN KRAUS & ANNE SPAFFORD

eno
publishers

Rain Gardening in the South
Copyright © 2009 Helen Kraus & Anne Spafford

CREDITS

All photographs by Helen Kraus, with the following exceptions: Figures 2 and 1-11 (a & b), by Kathy Mitchell; Figures 7, 2-3, and 2-4, by Anne Spafford; Chapter 1 front page, Figures 1-4, 1-6, and 1-12, by Richard Tyler; Figures 4-8 (a & b), by Ann Edwards; Figures 6-4 and 6-7, by Cherrie Tchir; Figure G-1, by Ted Bilderback; and Figure G-2, by Stuart Warren. All illustrations by Anne Spafford, with the following exceptions: Figures 3-3, 3-6, and 6-2, by Helen Kraus.

ISBN-10 0-9820771-0-6
ISBN-13 978-0-9820771-0-8
Library of Congress Control Number: 2008936738

Design and typesetting by Dave Wofford of
Horse & Buggy Press in Durham, North Carolina.

10 9 8 7 6 5 4 3 2

Eno Publishers
P.O. Box 158
Hillsborough, North Carolina 27278
www.enopublishers.org

ACKNOWLEDGMENTS

Many people have helped make this book what it is. We are very grateful to you all.

To...

Greg Kraus for all of his computer wizardry.

Rachel McLaughlin for her many hours of scanning expertise and chocolate.

Peggy Hickle, Dick and Judith Tyler and Barbara Horne for proofreading.

The students, faculty, and staff of the Department of Horticultural Science, North Carolina State University, and our friends and family for all their support and enthusiasm.

Elizabeth Woodman for her editing skills and passion and commitment to the environment.

Contents

INTRODUCTION

Is there anything more satisfying for a gardener than the sound of a slow, soaking rain? Is there anything more desperate than watching your beloved plants gasp for water in the middle of a drought—or drown in pooled water after a tropical depression?

As episodic droughts and floods remind us, water is the lifeblood of a garden. In terms of sheer weight, plants are 80 to 95 percent water. In fact, gardens are defined by how much water they require to support the plants growing in them.

Consider two extremes in gardens and their watering requirements: the xeric garden and the bog garden. Xeric plants thrive with little water and complete their life cycles quickly and/or store water in their leaves, stems, and roots. In xeric gardens, the soil is dry most of the time and any rain drains quickly from the soil. Bog gardens, on the other hand, don't require standing water, but their soil must remain moist. (Wetland gardens must have standing water—saturated soil—most of the time.)

FIGURE 1

Xeric garden   Rain garden   Bog garden   Wetland

least water ⟵——————————————————⟶ *most water*

FIGURE 2

A rain garden at Roanoke Island planted with ornamental grasses, black-eyed Susan, and joe-pye weed.

That brings us to rain gardens. Because of plant selection and filter bed preparation, rain gardens can tolerate periods when the soil is saturated *and* periods of dryness. In short, a rain garden differs from other gardens in the amount of time it can remain flooded—three days—and still thrive, and the extent of drought its plants can withstand.

As gardeners in the South well know, when it comes to rainfall, it's feast or famine. This region averages forty-four inches of rainfall annually, autumn being the driest season and summer—with thunderstorms that can deliver several inches of rain in a single evening—the wettest. These extremes can make traditional gardening a constant challenge, but also make our region a rain garden haven, because rain gardens thrive in both wet times and dry.

But what *is* a rain garden? Very simply, a rain garden is designed to capture rainfall flowing through your yard (known as runoff), store that water to nurture its plants, and cleanse runoff, thus removing the pollutants it carries with it.

Sounds good, doesn't it! Gardeners and city planners alike consider the rain garden to be the next great gardening practice that will define a landscape as being both beautiful and water-wise. Be the first house in your neighborhood to create one!

WATER—A FINITE RESOURCE

Nothing drives home the importance of preventing water pollution as this simple fact: All the water our planet will ever have is already here in some form. It is a finite resource, and gardeners everywhere can play an important role in protecting it.

Most of us think of the water cycle only in terms of how it affects our gardens and landscapes (see Figure 3). Rain falls and waters our gardens. If not enough rain falls, we irrigate.

Plants take up the water through their roots; the moisture then evaporates out of their leaves via transpiration and returns to the clouds. Rainfall that enters the soil can nurture plants or can drain below plant roots into the underground water reserves.

You may remember the water cycle you learned about as a child—the one with grass-munching cows grazing beneath billowy clouds, reliable gentle rains nurturing gardens and parklands, clear streams emptying into pristine rivers and then into the ocean, and great soil layered above a bountiful and pure underground water supply.

In the urban landscape, there's no such thing as a textbook water cycle. Instead, rainfall washes oil and other pollutants from roads and rooftops, and even sweeps up

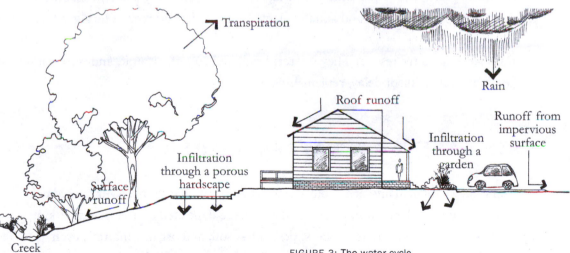

FIGURE 3: The water cycle

FIGURE 4: Hard surfaces—roofs and driveways—and traditional gardens are all sources of water pollution.

soil and fertilizers—mixing up a slurry of contaminated runoff. That highly polluted runoff then flows into municipal storm water collection systems. From there, it may go directly into streams and waterways or be directed to wastewater treatment systems to be cleaned before it returns it to the environment.

The idyllic water cycle we learned about in grade school also didn't take into account all the ways that humans tie up water so that it cannot return to the water cycle. When water is used for irrigation or is polluted as it moves through our urban environments, it must be cleaned up before it can be sent back into the water cycle. This detour results in a drop in lake and stream levels and a depletion in groundwater supplies.

Then again, if it's not cleaned up, and polluted runoff enters our waterways, we must deal with even more dire consequences. Much of the runoff contains nutrients that algae feed on. Soon, the lovely waterway—where you once dipped your toes or your children splashed—is green, slimy, and smelly. The algae, which aren't very smart, consume all the oxygen in the water. Fish and aquatic plants begin to die and reek. The algae thrive. Quite a mess.

Rain gardens to the rescue. They intercept polluted runoff, clean it, and return it to the water cycle without delay, replenishing water reserves.

RAIN GARDENS & WATER POLLUTION

Pollution exists in many forms, our gardens being just one source. Our everyday activities—driving vehicles (oil, grease, and antifreeze deposited on roads and parking areas), lawn and garden care (fertilizers, pesticides, soil, and organic matter), even walking the dog (feces and urine)—end up polluting our rivers, lakes, and coastal waters.

Exasperating pollution are the effects of our buildings and other hard surfaces. Because rain can't penetrate these impervious surfaces, it runs off them. Consider an area of undeveloped land (see Figure 5). Trees, understory vegetation, grasses are part of ecosystems that absorb water—water that is quickly returned to the water cycle.

After this same area of land is developed, much of this vegetation is replaced with hard surfaces—sidewalks, driveways, streets, rooftops (see Figure 6). Rain that falls on these surfaces might flow directly into waterways or be directed into wastewater facilities to be cleaned.

Even soil, innocuous as it seems, is a pollutant that gets swept away in runoff. With it go your mulch and fertilizers (nutrients you paid for!)—all wreaking havoc in the public waterways.

At this point, you may be thinking, "Well this doesn't happen in *my* yard. I fertilize responsibly. I irrigate responsibly. I mulch!"

Unfortunately, soil erosion happens with all soils—even soils from forests, where no synthetic fertilizers are applied and only natural decomposing organic matter provides nutrients for plant growth.

Fortunately, a well-functioning rain garden is very effective in preventing runoff, and in capturing and removing many pollutants. Metals such as zinc, copper, and lead

FIGURE 5: Area of land before development. Green areas are all vegetation.

FIGURE 6: Same area of land after development. Green areas are vegetation; black areas are hard surfaces.

can be absorbed by plants and filtered through the organic matter in the soil of the rain garden, removing 43 to 97 percent of these metals in runoff. Rain gardens also can remove 65 to 87 percent of the phosphorus and 15 to 92 percent of the nitrogen contained in runoff.

The effectiveness of a rain garden in removing pollutants

POLLUTANT	Source of pollutant	% Removed by rain garden
Copper	Roof shingles, oil, grease, soil	43–97%
Lead	Roof shingles, oil, grease, soil	70–95%
Zinc	Roof shingles, oil, grease, soil	64–95%
Phosphorus	Detergents, fertilizers, pet waste	65–87%
Total nitrogen	Fertilizer, pet waste, organic matter	49–67%
Calcium	Fertilizer	27%

SOURCE: U.S. EPA report on National Pollutant Discharge Elimination System storm water program. http://cfpub.epa.gov/npdes/stormwater/menuofbmps/index.cfm

How does a rain garden remove pollution and prevent scenes such as the one pictured in Figure 7? In a rain garden, pollutants can be absorbed by plant roots and either held in the plant or used by the plant for growth. Pollutants can be held in the soil by being bound to the soil particles or organic matter. Once attached to soil and organic particles, the pollutants are less likely to move downward toward groundwater supplies. Earthworms and soil microorganisms are able to ingest and neutralize pollutants.

FIGURE 7: Oily films and algae growth are both indicators of polluted water.

FIGURE 8: A retention basin at North Carolina State University in Raleigh.

Consider some of the rain garden's benefits:

- Captures, slows down, and encourages water to enter the soil where it can be used by plants, stored in the soil, and filtered on its way to the water table.

- Reduces runoff, especially that which flows into storm water collection systems.

- Uses rainfall to grow plants, thereby reducing the need for irrigation.

- Purifies the water that does end up in storm water collection systems by first filtering it, thus reducing the pollution that must be removed before the water can be used again.

To underscore the beauty of a rain garden, simply look at its alternative—the storm-retention basin (see Figure 8), used by large, commercial site planners to capture runoff. A retention basin is a hole in the ground that captures runoff from hard surfaces. Some have plantings around the edges (called a riparian buffer) that filter nutrients and other pollutants from the runoff. While effective in preventing water pollution, they are unsightly, best described as slime-filled cavities that make ideal mosquito breeding grounds.

Thus the need for rain gardens. Water-wise gardeners can limit their water use and minimize runoff—thereby dramatically reducing water pollution—and create a beautiful, cleaner environment.

FIGURE 9: A beautiful combination of woody trees and shrubs planted beside a rain garden tie the garden into the surrounding landscape.

HOW TO USE THIS BOOK

We hope you will find *Rain Gardening in the South* a user-friendly guide, offering a solid introduction to this important gardening movement, as well as an easy reference. The book begins by exploring rain gardening and what makes it a sound environmental practice and a water-wise way to garden. We then dig in (pardon the pun) and examine design and construction of a rain garden, and we take you along on our adventure of actually planting one.

As is obvious from its title, *Rain Gardening in the South* is a regional book. While the concepts and methodology of designing and constructing a rain garden are universal, the plant selections and soil mixture advice are particularly suited for our region. The plant lists included in Chapter Four are tried-and-true, tough plants that should thrive in a southeastern rain garden.

Whether you're new to rain gardening or have a yard full of such gardens, the troubleshooting chapter will be an important resource for getting the most out of your garden. We also have included lots of garden designs and plant lists for the shade, sun, and partial sun garden, as well as an appendix on soil considerations.

Realizing that readers approach books of this nature differently, we at times repeat material so that you can return to *Rain Gardening in the South* over and over again as an accessible resource. But we hope that you'll initially read it from cover to cover. It's a real page-turner. Plus, that way you won't miss any of our jokes.

Let's get started!

Helen & Anne

CHAPTER 1

RAIN GARDENS
The answer to drought, deluge, & water pollution

In one way or another, water defines a garden. Traditionally, gardeners have considered two important factors when designing a new garden: the amount of water that collects at the garden site, and/or the availability of irrigation.

Contemporary gardeners have another water issue to consider: pollution. Runoff from our gardens, yards, rooftops, and driveways flows into our streets, storm sewers, and, too often, into our waterways.

Nothing wrong with that, some gardeners might think. But they're wrong. Runoff is anything but clean (see the pollution table on page 14 in Introduction).

As the effects of runoff became apparent, towns and cities in the 1980s and 1990s tried to minimize runoff by requiring new developments to excavate storm-retention ponds. The results weren't pretty—huge rock-lined, mosquito-infested cavities in the landscape.

Then a group of urban planners in Maryland came up with a new idea—the rain garden. Actually, the idea was as old as the hills, but somehow had been lost through ages of urbanization. The garden—its fertilizers, mulch, and soil, all contributing to the runoff problem—could be designed to be part of the solution.

The rain garden essentially solves two major gardening problems—water supply and water pollution—and it does so in an attractive, non-retention-pond way. A rain garden is specifically structured to achieve those goals. Recessed usually three to six inches below the natural soil line, the rain garden draws in water, rather than allowing it to run across the property and become runoff. As water from nonporous surfaces—rooftops, driveways, parking lots—moves through a landscape, it is directed to and collects in the rain garden, where the water is stored in its soil and used to grow plants.

Water not needed for the rain garden's plants filters through the garden's porous soil mix, where pollutants in the water are removed—a process called filtration. The garden's organic matter and plant roots filter sediment and tie up pollutants, making the water safe to percolate to the groundwater.

Rain gardening is water-wise gardening. Water-wise gardeners are committed to using our finite water supplies carefully and preventing pollutants from ending up in waterways. Water-wise gardeners are good stewards of the earth and its resources.

THE DRY GARDEN

Southern gardeners face two common water challenges. The first is obvious to those who gardened through the devastating drought of 2007—too little water. Dry spells leave the traditional gardener with two choices: irrigate or garden with plants, such as succulents, that thrive in dry conditions.

Traditionally, a dry garden site requires a lot of mulch to preserve soil moisture or, when available, an irrigation system, preferably drip irrigation. Because of water restrictions in many communities and growing awareness of the need for water conservation, irrigation is not always an option.

Then there is plant selection for the dry gardens. Some xeric plants (e.g., cacti and succulents) have the ability to store water during wet periods and use that water during dry periods. However, they don't always flourish in the South. For example, many cacti can't survive the South's rainy winter months. Arid plants, such as artemisia (wormwood), can withstand extended periods of drought but also don't like humidity so don't grow well for southern gardeners.

A rain garden offers a perfect solution for a dry spot. Because it is slightly sunken, a rain garden captures rainfall and stores it in the soil until the plants need it.

Plant selection is also an important part of why a rain garden can thrive when rainfall is scarce. Rain garden plants are beautiful and tough—able to survive extended periods of drought without irrigation.

FIGURE 1-1: A newly planted rain garden planted with carex, irises, and dwarf bananas between the Apex Town Hall and community center.

THE WET GARDEN

Too much water in a garden also can be devastating.

Consider this situation: Rain falls on the roof, collects in the gutters, flows through the downspouts, then ponds several feet away from the home, creating a soggy mess where nothing will grow and even mulch floats away (see Figure 1-2). (There's nothing like having to retrieve your costly mulch from the neighbor's lawn after a good rain!)

A rain garden is a good solution for this type of site. Runoff from the downspout flows through a pipe buried underground, or on ground surface, and is directed away from the home's foundation. The water empties into a rain garden where it supports plant growth.

FIGURE 1-2

Left, runoff from a roof, ponding near a foundation.

Right, runoff directed into a rain garden through a drainage pipe attached to a downspout and buried in a ditch.

FIGURE 1-3: Rain garden one year after planting. A ground cover is used instead of an organic or inorganic mulch to prevent erosion and weed growth.

After a year of growth, the rain garden is flourishing, and the home's foundation is dry. No irrigation is needed to support the plant's growth in this rain garden.

Let's look at another landscape situation: The homeowners wanted a lawn where their children could play. But a lot of water flowed into their yard from their roof and the neighboring properties, causing soil erosion and ground too saturated for turf grass to survive.

Landscape contractors installed a series of drainage pipes throughout the lawn and from each downspout. The pipes pulled water from the soil and directed it toward the rain garden. Within the rain garden, swales were created and rocks placed to slow the water's velocity as it travels down the slope (see Figure 1-4).

With proper drainage, a beautiful lawn now grows there for the first time. Plantings of carex and ornamental grasses help the rain garden bridge the turf and wooded areas.

FIGURE 1-4 (on next page)
Rain garden connecting turf and wooded areas.

ANATOMY OF A RAIN GARDEN

Rain gardens are fairly easy and inexpensive to create. They have a defined structure made up of five basic components (see Figure 1-5).

First a depression is created, either by berming a sloped area or by digging down three to six inches and piling soil around the edges of the garden. A rain garden need not be excessively deep—only deep enough to capture a significant amount of water. To take care of heavy, frequent rain events, an overflow area should also be prepared to direct any excess water out of the rain garden without washing away the mulch and plants. This overflow area can be lined with living ground covers or rocks to prevent soil erosion.

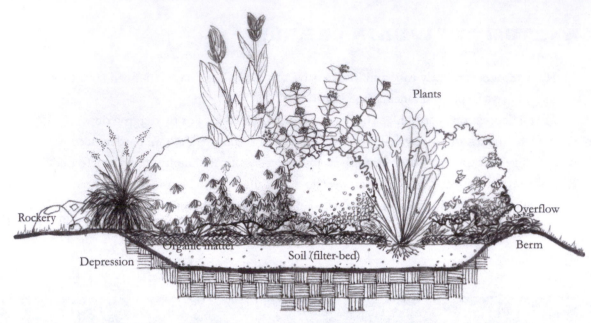

FIGURE 1-5: Cross-section of a rain garden showing the five major components.

Second, the soil of the rain garden needs to be addressed. The soil in a rain garden may need to be amended so that water can enter into (infiltrate) and drain through the soil quickly, thus creating a filter bed. (For those who don't stay up at night thinking about soil, see "The dirt on filter beds" in Chapter Three.)

When the soil in the rain garden is amended properly, runoff quickly infiltrates and doesn't pond on the surface. In a heavy rain, it may take up to three days for it to all seep into the filter bed. Gardeners should take every precaution to prevent water from standing for any longer than three days. Otherwise, you may be dealing with algae growth, mosquito breeding, and the possibility of overflow, should there be another rainfall. (By the way, mosquito larvae require seven to eight days to mature into the flying, biting daemons that take all the fun out of gardening.)

Third, and critical to all garden soils, is organic matter, added either as mulch or a soil amendment, such as compost. (Organic matter is a great gift idea, though not very wrap-able, for any of your gardening loved ones.) Not only does organic matter (also called humus) increase the soil's ability to absorb and drain water, it also fosters the proliferation of microscopic organisms and earthworms—vital to healthy soil and its ability to support plant growth and remove pollutants.

As long as it's been composted, any organic matter makes a good amendment; however, organic mulches should have large enough particles to prevent them from washing away during a heavy rainfall.

Fourth is plant selection. Plants are chosen that help remove pollutants, slow water movement across the soil, and return water back to the water cycle. Additionally, they support wildlife and are gorgeous.

Further, rain garden plants must be able to tolerate both short periods of flooding and extended periods of drought. Woody trees and shrubs, as well as a selection of perennial flowers, provide the filtration needed in a rain garden. (See Chapter Four, "Plantings," devoted to our one true love.) Although not addressed in *Rain Gardening in the South*, some annual plants will also thrive in a rain garden.

FIGURE 1-6: A flat area in a sloping rain garden, planted with various species of carex, slows water flow and lets it infiltrate the soil.

And *fifth*, some gardens use rocks to slow the water's velocity or create swales that allow water to collect and enter the soil.

Rock features can be designed to flow with the natural contours of the landscape, creating motion and visual interest. Rocks also can add beauty to the garden, although they don't fit every landscape. Nothing looks odder than a large rockery area without another rock in sight! If you have a rockless yard, consider other methods—for instance, ground covers—of slowing water movement into, through, and out of the rain garden. As with mulches, rocks in or around a rain garden need to be large enough to not wash away during a storm.

FIGURE 1-7

Runoff is directed through a shallow, rock-lined ditch down the hill, across the path, and into a meadow at the Giardino Alpinia in Italy.

RAIN GARDENS ABROAD & AT HOME

European gardeners design gardens that handle drought and deluge, going to great lengths to direct runoff toward plants and away from storm water collection systems. Many of their techniques are easily applied to landscapes in the South.

In the Giardino Alpinia near Stresa, Italy, a slight trough cut into a slope and lined with rock is planted with a sea of vegetation that directs rainfall down the hill, across a pathway, and then disperses the water into a meadow. There, it spreads out and nurtures the plants. Because the water in this garden is allowed to spread out laterally before it enters the meadow, it doesn't cause erosion.

FIGURE 1-8: Gravel walkway helps water drain into the ditches and then into the soil.

Porous walkways, instead of impervious surfaces, allow water to move into them instead of sheeting across. Ditches along the walk are lower than the walk's surface and lined in rock to prevent the walk's gravel from washing away (see Figure 1-8). The ditches also direct runoff to the garden.

FIGURE 1-9

Sloped area with drainage pipes and drain installed to direct runoff into this island planting around the base for a statue at Frederik Meijer Gardens and Sculpture Park.

At the Frederik Meijer Gardens and Sculpture Park in Grand Rapids, Michigan, water that runs down a steep slope from both the lawn and the parking lot is used for irrigating an island garden around the base of a statue (see Figure 1-9). By installing a series of drains and perforated pipe, the runoff is directed from this sloped area, soil erosion is prevented, the lawn thrives, and this island planting—which otherwise would have been very dry and difficult to support plant growth—becomes ready for a healthy garden. (The white fabric covering on the four-inch drainage pipe prevents soil from clogging the pipe.) Thus, an erosion problem is avoided and a garden space created.

There are many examples of beautiful rain gardens closer to home, including one near Asheville, North Carolina (see Figure 1-10), and one at the North Carolina Aquarium on Roanoke Island, Manteo (see Figure 1-11).

FIGURE 1-10: Roadside rain garden near Asheville, North Carolina.

FIGURE 1-11: Top, rain garden at the North Carolina Aquarium on Roanoke Island, the first year it was planted; and, below, three years later.

FIGURE 1-12: Sedge used to filter runoff in an informal rain garden.

MOVING ON

A rain garden is a biologically diverse ecosystem designed to utilize and filter rain that falls onto and moves through a landscape. Because of its plant selection, it also can withstand drought to a greater extent than can a traditional garden. The design of a rain garden requires examination of the entire landscape—its input and outputs. Water-wise gardening practices, such as mulching and drip irrigation, are made even more effective with the addition of the rain garden's filtration and removal of pollutants.

Next we look more closely at the design aspects that will help make your rain garden both functional and beautiful.

CHAPTER 2

DESIGNING A RAIN GARDEN

Let's get down to designing a rain garden. There are few *rules* about design. But there are myriad considerations. This chapter offers some guidelines that will help you plan a gorgeous rain garden.

Before you jump in and begin to dig and plant (we know you want to), take some time to analyze your yard. We mean, *really* analyze it.

PROPERTY ANALYSIS CHECKLIST

Have you ever planted something you later decided was in the wrong spot or too big or in too much sun? Mistakes happen, sometimes for the better, but we can avoid many errors with some early detective work.

Many great gardens begin on paper, analyzing existing structures, trees, other gardens. Because location is so essential to the success of a rain garden, we urge you to pick up a pencil and paper and start to sketch.

Roughly draw your house footprint, noting window and door locations, property lines, and any vegetation that isn't going anywhere (large, healthy trees, established slow-growing plants, etc.). Note significant views and unsightly ones you would like to screen.

Review the following property analysis checklist for additional notations that should be made on your map. Remember, none of this has to be drawn to scale—a rough sketch works just fine.

Water flow on property: Where does water enter the yard? Where does it leave? Are there areas that pond after a heavy rain or where washouts occur?

Slope of the ground: Are there flat areas where water collects? Are there steep areas where plant material, mulch, and/or soil might wash away during a heavy rain? Make sure that any re-grading you do results in water flowing away from *all* structures.

Sun/shade patterns: What areas receive morning light or full afternoon sun? Where is there dappled or partial shade or dark shade? Note areas that receive afternoon shade in the summer, but are exposed in the winter — some plants such as aucuba and other broadleaf evergreens don't like such extremes.

Important views: In which rooms do you spend the most time and do they have views of the yard? What about the views from your deck or patio? Could placing the rain garden in full view enhance these?

Existing significant vegetation: Small plants that may not work visually or technically in the rain garden can be transplanted to other places. Large plants, of course, are another matter. Be careful not to place your new rain garden too close to trees. Some tree species are very intolerant of digging around their roots. With others species, it will just be a tough, thankless job for whoever is doing the digging (*helloooooo brother-in-law!*).

Underground and overhead obstructions: Buried cables and pipes also need to be identified so they can be avoided. You don't want to accidentally hit something with a shovel while digging the garden's filter bed. It could cost plenty to get it fixed. Also, try to anticipate the height of your plants when they mature and whether they might grow into an overhead line, creating a pruning nightmare.

Taking time to analyze existing conditions will help you place the rain garden in the best possible location, select appropriate plants, and make sure you're spending your time, money, and energy well the first time!

WATER FLOW

Here's an obvious statement: For a rain garden to be effective, it must capture rainfall. To ensure that the garden is located where it will do just that, examine the path rain travels as it flows through your yard. You may need to stand in your yard during a rain (take an umbrella) or run a hose to watch where the water flows.

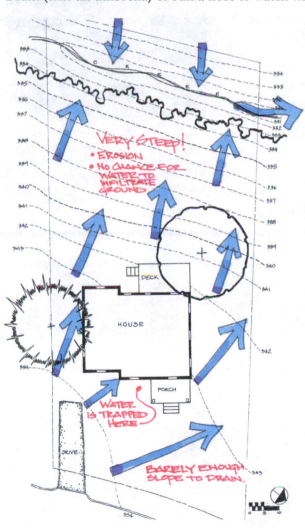

On the map of your yard, mark the water paths, as well as the points where water leaves your property and enters a storm water collection drain or runs onto your property from neighbors' yards and vice versa.

FIGURE 2-1: A map of Anne's property shows the general flow of water as it moves through her landscape. Several problem areas (standing water, steep slope) are indicated.

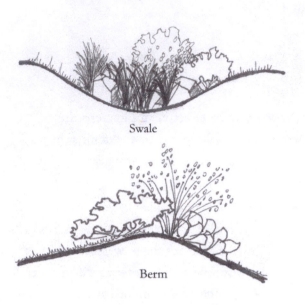

FIGURE 2-2: Diagram of a swale and a diversion berm.

FIGURE 2-3: A swale that collects water from a parking lot. This area could easily become a rain garden by amending the filter bed and choosing rain garden-friendly plants.

If water doesn't flow in the direction you want, you can divert it to a certain degree by building swales or berms to direct it toward the rain garden. (See Figure 2-2.)

FIGURE 2-4: A swale lined in rock and used to direct heavy rainfalls through this garden.

LOCATION, LOCATION, LOCATION

The best location for a rain garden is midway between the source of the runoff and the point where it enters the storm water collection system. This placement also allows any overflow from the rain garden to move through more vegetation before it leaves your property. However, a rain garden located anywhere that water can flow into it is a good location—definitely better than not having one!

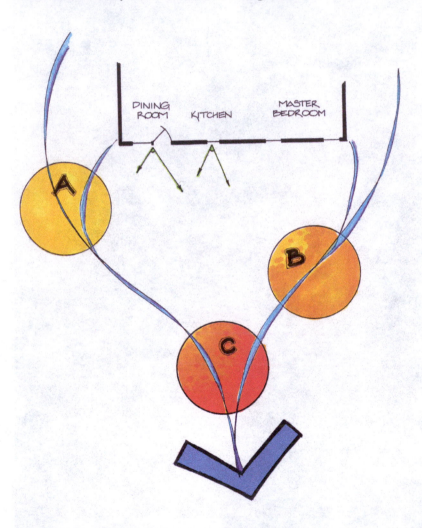

FIGURE 2-5: A bird's-eye view shows how runoff flows around the home's perimeter. Circles represent possible rain garden locations. **Circle A** would capture only some runoff; is too close to the foundation; can't be seen from the house. **Circle B** is visible from the house, but only captures runoff from one side of the house. **Circle C**, the best location, captures water from both sides, is visible, and is far enough away from the foundation.

Because of its high moisture content and potential pollution accumulation, a rain garden should be located at least ten feet from a home or wellhead. It also should be located at least twenty-five feet from a septic field.

Imagine a hard rain sheeting down a driveway, washing away residues that have collected there. Without the filtration provided by a rain garden, all that crud would flow into the storm water collection system or an open body of water.

Now picture this: Pollutant-laden runoff passes through a grassy area near the drive before entering a slightly sunken, beautiful rain garden full of perennial flowers and shrubs. The grassy buffer slows the water and pre-filters any soil and coarse organic debris that could clog the rain garden. The soil in the garden's filter bed encourages rapid infiltration, retains the water for the garden plants to utilize, and removes any pollutants. Meanwhile, the flowers in the rain garden thrive and provide season-long beauty. A pretty picture, isn't it?

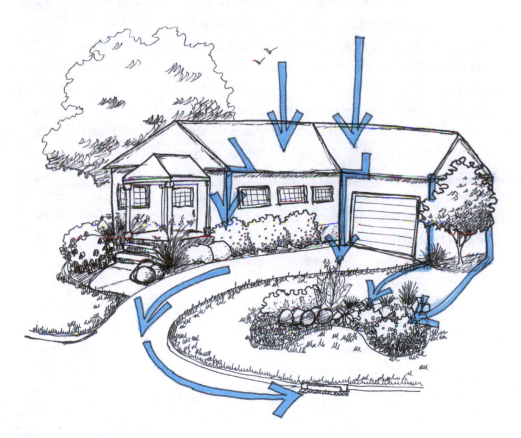

FIGURE 2-6: The flow of runoff in a yard with a driveway; and a possible rain garden site that would intercept runoff from hard surfaces.

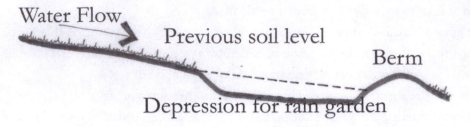

FIGURE 2-7: A rain garden installed on a slope.

On a slope, a rain garden is best located at the midway point (see Figure 2-7). There, the soil removed by digging the depression for the rain garden can be used to berm-up the lower side of the slope. Designing an overflow into the berm will allow excess water to flow through vegetation before it reaches the edge of your property.

But where can you place a rain garden in a flat, nondraining yard? With careful planning, water can be directed into the rain garden through four-inch perforated drainage pipes, buried underground. (See Figure 2-8.) The ditch, which needs to provide enough slope to move the runoff into the rain garden, should be at least ten inches deep at the point at which it flows into the rain garden and then slowly taper upward to the point at which it collects the runoff. The drainage pipe can be connected directly to the downspout of a gutter or to a collection drain installed where the runoff collects. (Landscape fabric covering the drainage pipe will prevent soil from clogging the pipe over time.) Because the pipe is perforated, water can seep into it anywhere along its length and then drain downhill toward the rain garden.

Unfortunately, some locations just aren't suitable for rain gardens. An already-wet spot is not a good place because the soil may already be so saturated that it cannot absorb more water. You can install drainage pipes in these areas and amend their soils to improve drainage; but wet areas may be better suited for bog gardens.

A very dry location with sandy soil probably isn't a good location either. Sandy soil requires large amounts of amendments that will retain water before the drainage rate of the filter bed will slow down enough to remove pollutants.

FIGURE 2-8 (from L to R): Drainage pipe in ditch; checking slope with a level; runoff deposited into rain garden; collection drain; "sock" on drainage pipe to prevent sediment from clogging it.

PUT IT IN CONTEXT

Whether you're starting from scratch (new home construction with zero landscaping, for instance) or reworking an old landscape, consider the design of the larger area (backyard and front yard). That way, your rain garden will look like a comprehensive, well thought out, and harmonious landscape. There's nothing more frustrating than realizing, *Oh, drats! We should have made the patio larger, planned for shade over here, incorporated more color out of the living room window. . . .* Spend time, money, and energy getting it right the first time!

Consider how you most often will see your rain garden. Will you be able to see it from your kitchen window? Will the best views be from the first floor or second? Will you usually be looking at it from afar or close up (or both)? Do you want to incorporate a small seating area next to it?

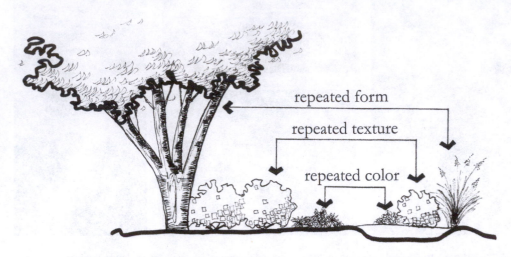

FIGURE 2-9: Repeated textures and other elements tie different segments into a cohesive garden.

Also, try to visualize the rain garden's relationship to other gardens in your yard. Do you want it to stand out as something separate or to blend harmoniously? Both approaches are fine, but you want to decide early on. For example, if you want the new rain garden to blend in, you may want to incorporate it into an existing planting area. Or, you can repeat some garden element from an existing garden—using the same plant, foliage color and/or texture, or even plant habit.

The diagrams opposite show different ways of incorporating variously shaped rain gardens into the landscape.

How the rain garden fits into your yard depends on the bed lines of your existing gardens. The rain garden should relate to those lines, either directly (by tying the rain garden in to an existing bed) or indirectly (by designing the rain garden's outline to follow the contours of adjacent garden beds).

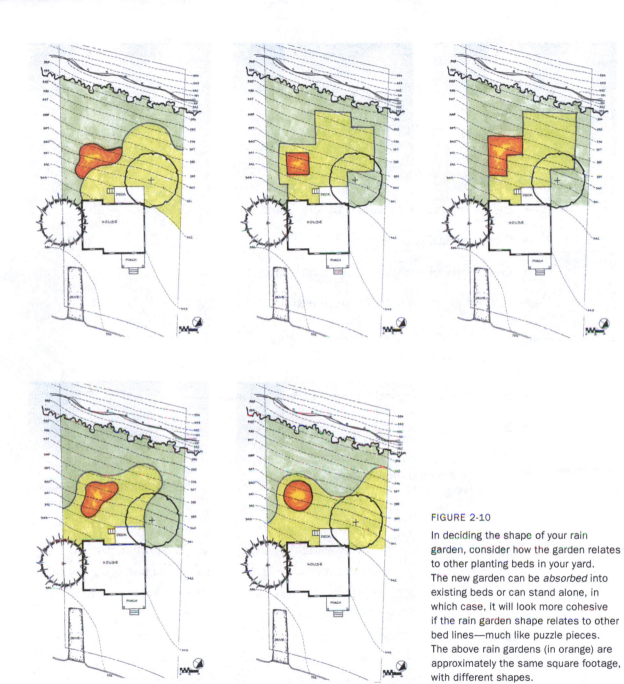

FIGURE 2-10

In deciding the shape of your rain garden, consider how the garden relates to other planting beds in your yard. The new garden can be *absorbed* into existing beds or can stand alone, in which case, it will look more cohesive if the rain garden shape relates to other bed lines—much like puzzle pieces. The above rain gardens (in orange) are approximately the same square footage, with different shapes.

GARDEN STYLE

Most of the rain garden examples we've shown are very naturalistic and informal. However, it's possible to design a formal one that may be well suited to a front yard rain garden. Consider the different characteristics of the two:

Informal garden

- Sweeping, gentle, curved, naturalistic, and/or organic bed lines.

- Asymmetrical plant groupings.

- Gentle mix of evergreens, deciduous plants, and perennials.

- Natural plant forms (not pruned into shapes).

Formal garden

- Straight or geometrically precise curved bed lines.

- Bilaterally symmetrical planting.

- Plants sheared or pruned into geometric shapes.

- More evergreens (not always the case).

What makes a garden formal? you might ask. Good question! Formal gardens often are designed with bilateral symmetry—one side of the garden mirroring the other. If you draw a line through the plan on the next page from the top left corner to the lower right corner, you'll see (if you haven't already) that the two halves are identical. The shrub perimeter, emphasizing the rectangular geometry, also makes it formal. Daylilies are massed in rectangular blocks instead of a more naturalistic sweep.

Formal gardens often include water features. In this planting scheme, a (dwarf) weeping bald cypress is used to mimic a cascading fountain.

FIGURE 2-11: Example of a formal rain garden—A. inkberry (sheared); B. daylily; C. 'Hummingbird' Clethra; D. yarrow; E. false indigo; F. aster; G. weeping bald cypress; H. cardinalflower; I. butterfly weed.

DESIGN & MAINTENANCE

The desire for low maintenance gardens is a given these busy days. No one wants to be pruning, weeding, mowing, deadheading, edging, mulching, and weed-eating every spare minute. As much as we love spending time in our gardens, we have places to go, things to do! Besides, our goal is to enjoy our gardens.

Here are some tips to ensure your rain garden is low maintenance:

- If your rain garden abuts turf, insert edging to keep the turf from encroaching on the garden.

- If you have to mow up to the border of your rain garden, remember that tight arcs and corners are hard to mow! Having to trim or weed-eat: bad. Mowing in just one pass: great!

FIGURE 2-12: A rain garden composed of only woody plants that are disease- and insect-resistant and require little pruning.

- Not sure if a bed line will be easy or hard to mow around? Lay out a section of garden hose to simulate the proposed bed line. Test by running your mower along the line (we suggest doing this with the mower *off*, unless you want a shredded hose).

- If your rain garden is large, allow yourself one (or a few) mini pathway for easy access to hard to reach areas for weeding.

- Sweeps (groupings) of plants are less maintenance. If you're a follower of the "one of this, one of that" school of gardening, remember that each one of those plants may have different care requirements!

- Leave enough room for plants to grow and attain their full width. Overcrowded plants become stressed, which leads to competition for nutrients, encourages disease, and pretty much puts out an *Eat Here!* sign for pests.

MOVING ON

Now that the rain garden's location has been determined and its context within the landscape considered, it's time to determine its size.

We also need to examine the real workhorse of the rain garden—the filter bed. Without a well-developed filter bed, the rain garden will not be successful either aesthetically or in removing pollutants.

CHAPTER 3

LAYING THE GROUND WORK

It's all about the prep work. As we stressed in Chapter Two, successful rain gardens require planning. We now move on to calculate the garden's size and the best way to prepare the soil. Ideally, the amount of water flowing into the area you've designated for the garden should determine the size of your rain garden. That calculation isn't rocket science, but it does require a little math, and we provide just the tools to help you.

Analyzing the garden's soil (the all-important filter bed) and figuring out how best to amend it are critical preliminary steps to take before the first plant is planted.

To illustrate these important basics in rain gardening, we run outside and play in the dirt (after we finished our rain gardening homework). Read all about our adventures in "Rain garden in action."

WATER MOVEMENT IN SOIL

Rainfall usually moves into the soil (infiltrates) in the soft areas of a landscape (e.g., lawn, mulched garden beds), preventing runoff. Consider the rain's journey once it falls on your roof (the major hard surface of most home landscapes): It flows into the gutters and is then directed through downspouts, which are usually connected to drainage pipes or a gravel channel at the foundation. (See Figure 3-1.) Ideally, this runoff should be carried through the drainage system to a point at least ten feet from the foundation. Nonperforated drainage pipe should be used for that ten-foot ride, at which point perforated pipe can be used to distribute runoff throughout the landscape or to direct it toward a rain garden.

If a home doesn't have gutters, runoff can cause extensive soil erosion around the foundation, which isn't good for the environment or the foundation. A wet foundation can result in a leaky basement, uneven settling of the foundation resulting in cracks, and termite activity.

To prevent soil from washing away, it's important to slow surface runoff on its way to the rain garden. Soil carried into the rain garden by runoff will clog the garden; you then will have to re-dig the filter bed to make it functional again. Digging once when you're creating the garden is fun (maybe). Digging twice is not.

Slowing the water can be done by directing runoff across lawn areas, rocks, gravel, plants, or anything that can reduce its velocity. This also helps prevent erosion around the edges of the garden. (Fabric can be placed under rock along the edges as an added protection against soil erosion.)

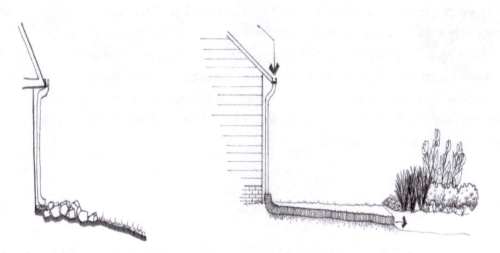

FIGURE 3-1: Two methods of transferring roof runoff away from a foundation—either by passing the runoff through rocks or through a buried drainage pipe.

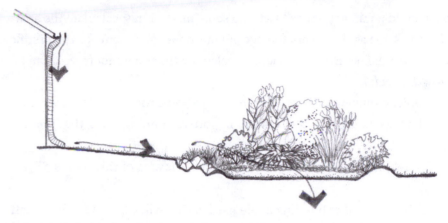

FIGURE 3-2: Typical design of a rain garden constructed to capture roof runoff.

At times, rainfall will exceed the rain garden's capacity. Fortunately, for the integrity of our water supplies, most pollutants are washed from our roofs or driveways during the first inch of rainfall, which should not exceed a rain garden's capacity. Additional rain that overflows the garden most likely will be less polluted. However, this is water lost to the rain garden. And overflow can damage borders and berms around the garden. So plan a pathway that directs the excess water to other landscape plantings.

SIZE MATTERS

Determining the length and depth of a rain garden can be tricky. The short and easy answer is—any size is better than no rain garden. The longer, harder answer is—the rain garden's depth is determined by the garden's soil; the length and width (*depth* x *length* x *width = garden volume*) are determined by the amount of water you want to capture, plus your budget and energy level. Obviously, the bigger and deeper the rain garden, the more water it will catch.

To be effective as a pollution filter, the rain garden volume should be between 5 to 10 percent of the impervious area (e.g., rooftops, driveways) that drains into it. It needs to be recessed three to six inches below the natural grade. (See Figure 3-2.) The critical factor is that the rain garden be able to drain in two to three days. As we've mentioned, standing water serves as a mosquito breeding ground.

So, how big should a rain garden be? Let's do some math. First, calculate the area of your roof. It's the same as the square footage of your one-storey home or the first floor of your multiple-storey home. But if you need to calculate the square footage, it can be calculated as *length* x *width.*

Take, for example, a simple, ranch-style home with a gable roof that slopes toward the front and back of the house. Rainfall collects in gutters running along the front and back of the roof.

The eave is 85 feet long and the span is 30 feet wide. The area of this roof is *85 ft. x 30 ft. = 2,550 ft.²*.

Let's set an ambitious goal of building a rain garden that will capture all the runoff from the front half of the roof. Divide the roof's square footage in half (*2,550 ft.² ÷ 2 = 1,275 ft.²*).

Another factor we want to take into account in calculating the rain garden for this particular yard is the home's concrete surface. The driveway is 12 feet wide and 30 feet long (*12 ft. x 30 ft. = 360 ft.²*).

Because we strive to be excellent stewards of our water supplies, we want all the rainwater that runs off these hard surfaces to collect in a rain garden near the street in front of this house.

In this example, half the roof and the entire drive equal 1,635 square feet of impermeable surface (*1,275 ft.² + 360 ft.² = 1635 ft.²*). To be able to collect a 1-inch rainfall, divide the impermeable area by 20 (a constant) for a 6-inch deep rain garden to calculate the ideal size (*1,635 ft.² ÷ 20 = 80 ft.²*). So, with roughly 1,600 square feet of impermeable area and a 6-inch-deep rain garden to capture a 1-inch rainfall, the rain garden needs to be roughly 80 square feet—translating to a 7-foot by 12-foot area or an 8-foot by 10-foot area.

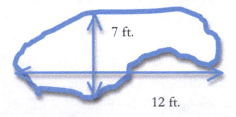

7 ft.

12 ft.

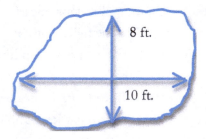

8 ft.

10 ft.

FIGURE 3-3: Sizing a rain garden.

Math challenged? Here's a table that you can use to determine the size of a rain garden that can capture a one-inch rain.

Required rain garden size to capture an inch of rain

Impermeable surface area	Required size of rain garden (6" deep)	Potential rain garden dimensions (ft. x ft.)	Required size of rain garden (3" deep)	Potential rain garden dimensions (ft. x ft.)
800 ft.²	40 ft.²	4 x 10, 5 x 8, 6 x 7	80 ft.²	7 x 12, 8 x 10, 9 x 9
1000 ft.²	50 ft.²	5 x 10, 6 x 8	100 ft.²	7 x 15, 10 x 10
1200 ft.²	60 ft.²	4 x 15, 5 x 12, 6 x 10, 8 x 8	120 ft.²	10 x 12, 8 x 15
1400 ft.²	70 ft.²	5 x 14, 7 x 10	140 ft.²	10 x 14, 7 x 20
1600 ft.²	80 ft.²	7 x 12, 8 x 10, 9 x 9	160 ft.²	8 x 20, 10 x 16
1800 ft.²	90 ft.²	6 x 15, 7 x 13, 8 x 12, 9 x 10	180 ft.²	9 x 20, 10 x 18, 12 x 15
2000 ft.²	100 ft.²	7 x 15, 10 x 10	200 ft.²	10 x 20, 14 x 15
2500 ft.²	125 ft.²	8 x 16, 10 x 13	250 ft.²	10 x 25, 13 x 20, 15 x 17
3000 ft.²	150ft.²	10 x 15, 12 x 13	300 ft.²	10 x 30, 15 x 20
3500 ft.²	175 ft.²	9 x 20, 12 x 15	350 ft.²	14 x 25, 18 x 20
4000 ft.²	200 ft.²	10 x 20, 14 x 15	400 ft.²	16 x 25, 20 x 20
5000 ft.²	250 ft.²	10 x 25, 13 x 20, 15 x 17	500 ft.²	20 x 25

Table reprinted from Rain Garden Booklet (http://www.bae.ncsu.edu/topic/raingarden/material.htm), used with permission of Bill Hunt.

Note: A shallow (three-inch) rain garden must be twice as large as a deeper (six-inch) rain garden. Except in heavy clay soils, a six-inch deep rain garden is the best option, filling less of the landscape. With a heavy clay soil, it can be a real challenge to amend the soil sufficiently to develop a deep filter bed; so a larger, shallower rain garden may be the best choice. And if the space is available, a three-inch deep rain garden will be effective. The same amount of work is required—either dig deeply over a small area or not so deeply over a larger area.

RAIN BARREL VERSUS RAIN GARDEN

While we're messing around with numbers, let's consider what's involved in catching runoff from the roof in a rain barrel, instead of directing it to the rain garden. With a one-inch (*1 in. = 0.08 ft.*) rain captured in the gutters on half of this home's roof (1,275 ft.²), the calculation goes like this: *1,275 ft.² x 0.08 ft. x 7.5 gal/ft.³ = 765 gallons of water* (7.5 gallons in one cubic foot). That's a big barrel! And, that's only one one-inch rainfall.

We don't discourage the use of rain barrels at all. We merely point out that they are not the only solution to rainfall runoff and drought issues. In some cases, a rain garden might not work (e.g., a site too close to the home's foundation). Plus, a rain barrel offers a great source for all those spot-watering needs. (For more on rain barrels and other rain harvesting methods, see Chapter Six, "Other water-wise gardening options.")

THE DIRT ON FILTER BEDS

A rain garden's filter bed (also called soil mix) allows water to quickly enter (infiltrate) the garden's soil and then be used by the plants. The soil binds pollutants, preventing them from moving down into groundwater supplies. Without a well-designed filter bed, water may pool—attracting mosquitoes and causing plant roots to rot.

Great filter beds, particularly in the South, begin with soil amendment. Filter bed soil must be designed with both coarse-textured particles that let water enter the soil and finer-textured particles that hold the water for plant use. The coarse-textured soil needs to be on top of finer-textured soil to prevent the latter from eroding. (See Figure 3-4.)

Additionally, the filter bed needs to be three to six inches below the natural grade of the landscape and six to twelve inches deep.

To understand the importance of soil amendments, let's consider two contrasting soil types—clayey and

FIGURE 3-4: Soil system with organic mulch (coarse-textured particles) over finer-textured soil particles.

FIGURE 3-5: Calculating soil amendments.

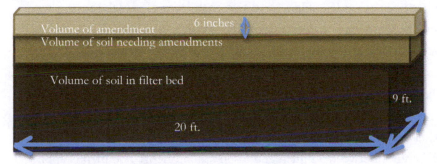

FIGURE 3-6: Layering soil amendment.

sandy. Clayey soils hold water well, requiring rain or irrigation only once every seven to ten days. However, clayey soils do not have rapid infiltration rates (0.05 inches per hour). In other words, clayey soils have the water-retention properties needed for a filter bed, but lack the ability to allow runoff to move into the soil quickly. Therefore, soil amendments with large particle size (big chunks), such as compost or pea gravel, need to be mixed into the clayey filter bed.

Sandy soils, on the other hand, do not hold water well, needing frequent watering (every two to three days). But sandy soil has infiltration rates (0.25 inches per hour) roughly five times faster than clay. Sandy soil needs to be amended to improve its water retention, which involves mixing small particle-size bits, such as compost, into it. (See "Soil basics" on the next page.)

By now you're probably wondering why we began this chapter promising that constructing a rain garden wasn't that hard, and now we're talking about designing soil! Doesn't that involve dinosaur time and the movement of glaciers? Fortunately, only the upper six to twelve inches of soil need to be amended to build a great filter bed. You can do that by using a tiller, a digging fork, or a plain old shovel.

Soil amendments should be the starting point of *any* garden. Besides, gardening becomes much easier and a lot more fun when done in a beautifully prepared soil.

Typically, the upper layer of soil needs to be amended by 25 to 50 percent; so we will need to do a bit more math. If your rain garden is twenty feet long, nine feet wide, and you want to amend the top twelve inches (one foot), the volume of soil you want to amend is *20 ft. x 9 ft. x 1 ft. = 180 ft.³* (see Figure 3-6). A 50 percent amendment means that you need to spread *180 ft.³ x 0.50 = 90 ft.³* of organic matter six inches (*1 ft. x 0.50*) deep over the surface of the garden, and then till it or dig it into the soil. It is often easier to mix in the amendment in three- or four-inch additions.

After the soil has been amended, add a good two-inch layer of mulch to the filter bed. Mulches increase infiltration and decrease weed growth. Any mulch, organic or inorganic, will work, although organic mulches also add organic matter to the soil.

Mulch has to be heavy enough not to wash away during a rain. Shredded tire mulch, pine straw, pine bark nuggets, and pine bark are generally too light for a rain garden. Mulches with a mixture of big and small particles, such as shredded bark and ground leaves, nest together and don't wash away as easily.

What is the difference between a mulch and a soil amendment? A mulch is applied on top of the soil and doesn't have to be composted (aged); a soil amendment is mixed into the soil and must be composted if it is organic (carbon-based).

SOIL BASICS

Soil is a system of large and small bits of rock with gaps between them. These gaps, called pores, can be filled with either water or air—big gaps filled with air and small gaps with water. Plant roots need both air and water.

Picture a large wood box filled with basketballs. Between the balls are gaps. The box is like a garden, the basketballs being the soil particles and the gaps the soil's pores.

Now imagine a box stacked with square dinner plates. If you pour a bucket of water over the plates, the water would run down the stack, from plate to plate, and eventually drain out the bottom of the box.

If you pour the same bucket over the basketballs in another box, the water would quickly flow through the large gaps between the balls and out the box.

Clayey soils are like the box of dinner plates, while sandy soils are like the box of basketballs.

Now imagine a wood box filled with basketballs, plates, and some sponges. If this were soil, the multiple-sized and -shaped soil particles (basketballs and plates) would create a mixture of pores, big and small, to provide both air and water; the sponges wedged between the soil particles would hold water.

RAIN GARDEN IN ACTION

The Kraus House backyard doesn't have a great deal of slope (see Figure 3-7); but when it rains, especially in the winter when the landscape's vegetation is not as thick, water sheets across the lawn and down a woodchip-covered path toward the house. The result—the mulch ends up in the driveway!

Rain garden to the rescue!

We select a spot in the backyard where we can direct the runoff into a rain garden before it reaches the woodchip walkway. This will be a small rain garden, roughly ten feet by six. (An existing rain garden in the front yard catches most of the runoff from the roof and driveway.)

FIGURE 3-7
Slope in the Kraus house backyard.

To prepare the backyard bed, we start by killing the existing grass and microstegia invading an area of the backyard. (Microstegia is a hard-to-control weed often best controlled with an herbicide.)

Next, we dig out twelve inches of soil from the center of the rain garden. As we do this, we set the soil on a tarp, where it later can be amended. We slope the sides of the garden, so the water can gradually drain into the garden. We build a berm on the low side of the garden to stop the water flow (see Figure 3-10).

Once the digging is done, we begin mixing—blending the soil amendments. Considering the dimensions of the garden, we remove 60 cubic feet of soil (*10 ft. x 6 ft. x 1 ft. = 60 ft.³*). The soil already drains pretty well, so we amend it at the rate of 25 percent. We purchase 15 cubic feet of organic matter, in this case composted cow manure (calculating square footage times the percent of amending—*60 ft.³ x 0.25 = 15 ft.³*).

When exploring your favorite local garden supplier for compost, keep a few things in mind. First, any compost is good, as long as it has been composted well, meaning it has a rich, earthy smell and is not sopping wet.

Second, under absolutely no circumstance do you want to buy topsoil! This is one of the few things in life—right up there with sticking your finger in an electrical socket—you should never do.

You're probably wondering, What's up with that? There are at least two good reasons not to buy topsoil. First, you never know where it's been. It may be full of weed seeds just waiting for some sun and water to germinate and grow. Give a weed an inch and it will take a mile, no fertilizer required.

Second, you never know who its parent rocks were. Soil is a system assembled for drainage, an assemblage based on a specific layering of soil particles of contrasting sizes—large over small. An icing of a different texture is nice on a cake but not in a soil. If you spread soil of a much smaller texture (the only polite way to describe bagged topsoil) on top of your soil, water will not be able to enter your garden's soil. Result: a sloppy mess! (See Appendix, "A soil primer," and "Soil basics," earlier in this chapter.)

FIGURE 3-8: The killing of the weeds.

FIGURE 3-9: The digging of the bed—for now.

FIGURE 3-10: The building of the berm.

FIGURE 3-11
Cow manure spread over the
base of the filter bed.

Getting back to soil amendment, we spread two inches of composted cow manure over the soil and work it into the base of the filter bed to a depth of four inches. Then we spread two inches of soil on top of this amended base and add two more inches of compost. We mix it all with a digging fork.

At this point, we've amended 4in. + 4in. = 8 in. of soil in the filter bed, which has been recessed four inches below the original grade (remember—we dug down twelve inches). Yes, we have some leftover soil (four inches to be exact), which is used to fill in low spots. (Because this is the yard's native soil and not a store-bought topsoil, it's okay to spread around.)

If you have a larger rain garden and more soil to amend, you may want to take a different approach. Spread two inches of amendment over the soil surface before any digging begins. Using a digging fork or tiller, mix the amendment into the soil. Dig out the amended soil and start forming the berm. Spread two more inches of amendment, mix, dig, and form the berm. Once the berm is completed, you can mix in the rest of the amendment.

The result of all this hard work is a beautiful, fluffy soil with a large diversity of soil particle sizes and organic matter that will have great infiltration, drainage, and water-retention abilities. Any plant's dream come true and a great pollution filter.

Back to the Kraus rain garden: Once the filter bed's soil is mixed, it's time for more shoveling. This is why gardening is good exercise. We form a berm along the front edge of the garden and curve it around the left side of the garden to direct the runoff into the garden along this path (see Figures 3-12 and 3-13). We use some retaining-wall blocks to

FIGURE 3-12
Rain garden filter bed finished.

FIGURE 3-13
Water flow directed into rain garden.

support the berm and supply some resistance so the berm's soil won't wash away. We choose blocks because the Kraus yard doesn't have rocks, and the blocks tie into those used around the patio area.

To get to this point takes us the better part of a day and a fair amount of sweat. (We also have to explain to the two Kraus children why we dug all the dirt out of the garden only to put it back in!)

FIGURE 3-14: Plants arranged and ready for planting.

Now we are ready for planting! As we mentioned, the runoff moves quickly through the lawn and washes away the Kraus House mulch. To help slow the movement of water into the garden, we select ornamental grasses, crested iris, and sedges for the edges of the garden (see Figure 3-14). A golden bald cypress adds some height to the plantings, its golden foliage blending nicely with the carex and little zebra miscanthus.

We also add some low-growing shrubs that, with the grasses, will give winter structure to the garden. We choose several perennials that will flower throughout the summer and even a weeping river birch that will eventually hang over the pathway and inflow.

We arrange the plants by size and height. Since this garden will be viewed from the front and back, we arrange taller and shorter plants throughout the garden to give varying heights and interest.

On the opposite page is the rain garden just after planting and with two inches of hardwood mulch spread between the plants (see Figure 3-15); following that is a photo of the same garden three months later (see Figure 3-16).

FIGURE 3-15: Just after planting and mulching.

FIGURE 3-16: Three months after planting. The plants include iris, sanguisorba, a variety of carex, dwarf fothergilla, and maidenhair grass.

MOVING ON

Planning and preparation are essential to the success of a rain garden. The goals of capturing water, filtrating pollution, and successfully establishing garden plants need to be kept clearly in mind during the planning and preparation stages. Shortcuts will result in less than satisfactory results or an outright failure.

Next we will explore plant selection and planting techniques. We all garden because we love plants—and so, *finally,* let's talk plants!

CHAPTER 4

PLANTINGS

You've picked the size, location, and shape of the rain garden. The hard physical labor is done: The filter bed has been created, the soil amended, the berm built. Now the fun part begins—selecting, placing, and planting plants.

DISPELLING GARDEN MYTHS

First, it's important to dispel two huge garden myths. The first concerns drought-tolerant plants. These plants are great when we are indeed *in* a drought; but in a typical year, the South receives around forty-four inches of rainfall. When our rainfall is normal, drought-tolerant plants don't fare so well, tending to suffer from rot and slowly die.

Another myth, in our opinion, is that "native is *always* better." Indigenous plants are not always the best choice. We like to plant a mix of natives and non-natives for the following reasons:

- Using only natives would be great, *if* we were dealing with native, non-urbanized conditions. But urban landscapes tend to be hotter because of our hardscape surfaces—roads, driveways, parking lots, rooftops. Too often, native soil has been altered or removed, thereby affecting water, oxygen, and nutrient availability. Urban humans create pollution, which is a challenge for some plants.

- To be at their best, native plants should be grown in their preferred native habitat. Many homeowners have flowering dogwoods planted in full sun, in compacted soil, and surrounded by turf. Even though these are native trees, they often struggle, because they prefer partial shade, such as at the edge of woods or in understory forest conditions, with lots of organic matter in the soil.

- Using native plants does not guarantee a fail-safe garden. Any newly installed plant, native or not, needs to be cared for until it has grown roots into the garden's soil. Additionally, our native plants aren't immune to pests and diseases. Not to pick on the gorgeous flowering dogwood again, but dogwood anthracnose is a huge problem, wiping out native dogwood plantings as we write. Many non-native, hybrid dogwoods are resistant to that devastating disease.

- There's a huge, beautiful palette of non-natives that grow well in the South. Many of these plants are considered garden staples. Imagine the Southeast without the crape myrtle or the Indian azalea. Neither is native, but they're tough and perform well for us.

Don't misunderstand. We're not against using native plants. Some of our favorite plants are natives, such as *Calycanthus floridus* (sweetshrub) and *Iris pseudacorus* (yellow flag)—which also happens to be *fabulous* in rain gardens although it might spread a bit. Probably the best argument *for* using native plants is that they provide food for our native wildlife.

FIGURE 4-1

Muhlenbergia and *Helianthus* mix and mingle, creating great contrast in texture and color.

IN THE ZONE

Before you pick your first plant, think zones: hydrozone, heat zone, hardiness zone. Knowing the zones in which you live will make all the difference in determining whether your rain garden is lush and effective or a failed experiment.

Hydrozone

A water-wise landscape divides areas of the landscape into different hydrozones, which are groupings of plants with similar water needs. Low-water-use hydrozones include established trees, shrubs, and some perennial flowers. These plants, once established, can go a month or possibly even longer without rainfall or irrigation. Turf grasses can also fit into a low-water-use hydrozone, but only if the lawn—typically a high-water-use hydrozone—is allowed to go dormant (turn brown) during dry periods.

Keeping lawns and other high-water-use plants green and growing during dry spells requires heavy irrigation. A high-water-use hydrozone often is designed for a heavily traveled area, such as near a front door or a deck. The rest of the yard can be landscaped with low-water-use gardens and be just as beautiful as thirstier hydrozones.

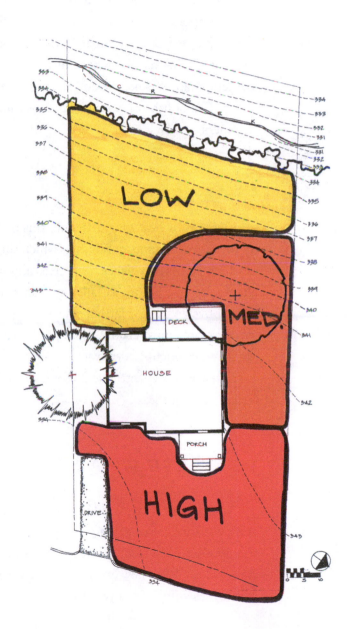

FIGURE 4-2: Hydrozones in the landscape diagram from Chapter Two (p. 35). Red indicates a high-water-use hydrozone (front yard, high-visual impact); orange, a medium-water-use hydrozone (transition pathway to backyard, still visible from the street); and yellow, a low-water-use hydrozone (perfect for a rain garden that can be enjoyed from the house).

Hardiness zone

Hardiness zones are determined by the average annual minimum temperatures. The Southeast falls between hardiness Zones 7 and 9. The higher the zone number, the higher the average cold temperature. For example, the average minimum temperatures of hardiness Zone 7 fall between 0°F and 10°F; whereas, low temperatures in hardiness Zone 9 range between 20°F and 30°F.

It's important to know the specific hardiness zone for your area to prevent your garden plants from freezing to death. A simple search of the Internet will provide you with the USDA hardiness zone map for your area. Keep in mind that the minimum low temperature is not the only determinant of a plant's success—humidity is also a key factor. The Southeast, with its humid summers, also affects plant selection. Speaking of summers. . .

Heat zone

Know your heat zone. After all, this is the Southeast. Heat zones are determined by the average number of days in which the temperature exceeds 86°F—the temperature at which plants experience heat stress and their growth slows dramatically or stops altogether. The Southeast falls between Zones 6 through 9 with an average of 45 to 150 days above 86°F. The farther south you go, the more days above 86°F you and your garden plants must endure. Rain gardens are a perfect way to supply those heat-stressed plants with much-needed water.

Later in this chapter, we do some detective work and compile a list of plants that do well in the Southeast.

DECIDING WHAT TO PLANT

After you've determined your zone specifications, you'll have a broad menu of plant choices. Great looking, long-lasting gardens are planted according to the specifics of the site—sun or shade, soil pH, water availability. You've heard the phrase "right plant, right place." Well, how can you choose the right plants when rainfall amounts fluctuate, sometimes wildly, from year to year?

FIGURE 4-3: Some annuals work well in a rain garden. Here is a beautiful combination of textures with the delicate flowers of the annual cat's whiskers set against the coarser-textured leaves of elephant ear and palmetto.

Easy—create a garden environment that captures rainfall, *and* choose plants that thrive in both wet and dry conditions. Plants need different amounts of water, and they experience and exhibit signs of water stress—caused by either very dry or very wet growing conditions—in different ways.

Plants in a rain garden are both drought-tolerant and able to withstand short periods of flooding. The plants may not flower and grow as much during times of water stress. Too, they may wilt or turn a duller shade of green. But they'll flower again and resume growing when the stress is removed.

Plants in a rain garden are more than just tough. They also absorb water and nutrients, removing pollutants before they end up in our water supplies. And, if that isn't enough, their flowers and foliage also add beauty to the landscape.

Don't underestimate the value of foliage when selecting rain garden plants. Whether green or variegated, deciduous or evergreen, leaves add interest to a garden longer than do flowers. Perennial plants—plants that die back, then return year after year—usually flower once a year, and even then, not for long. The rest of the year they build and store energy for their next reproductive event. That is what flowers do for a plant—lure a pollinator, to begin reproduction.

Mix up your rain garden and choose plants with different form and texture. A mixture of plants both woody (stems and leaves, sometimes evergreen, that remain alive and above ground year-round) and herbaceous (above-ground parts die and no visible growth occurs in the winter) adds variety and interest to the rain garden. Many deciduous woody plants look great in the winter. The overall form and flow of the garden change as herbaceous plants grow, die back, and then regrow.

ARTFUL PLANT COMPOSITION

We could write volumes about plant composition, but then you'd be stuck reading a book instead of working in your garden. Besides, aesthetics are highly personal. You love Monet. Your neighbor loves Picasso. There's no right and wrong. However, a few guidelines may save you several seasons' worth of trial and error:

Overlap plant masses

Overlapping plant groupings is visually appealing. Think of it this way: It often looks disjointed to have one massing completely stop and another begin. Instead, strive to overlap the ends of massings, so plant groupings *hug* each other.

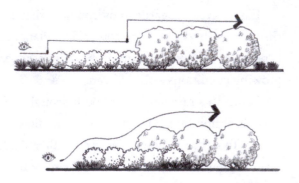

FIGURE 4-4: Overlapping plant massings.

FIGURE 4-5: A planting plan for a sunny location: A. iris; B. Japanese spirea; C. dwarf nandina; D. mock-orange; E. winterberry; F. aster; G. maidenhair grass; H. American beautyberry; I. redtwig dogwood; J. dwarf yaupon holly; K. carex; L. canna; M. iris; N. yarrow; O. crocosmia; P. Kirilow indigo; Q. Japanese barberry.

Plants in the sun garden plan above are found on the plant list later in this chapter. Note that most of the massings overlap—establishing a relationship between one another.

"Plant in odd numbers only"

You may have heard this before. But plants don't necessarily grow in odd numbers in nature. We're not sure where this odd-number predilection comes from. Perhaps our brains work in ways, that are, well . . . odd! When we look at a pairing of the same plants, our brains automatically split the massing in two groups of one and interpret it as a formal composition; so a pairing of plants can often look contrived. Planting in odd numbers is generally a good rule of thumb. A common exception is when the individual plant forms are lost when grouped together, and you can't really tell how many there are.

When you scrutinize the sun garden plan on page 71, you may notice a pair of inkberries. But look again. Notice a third pulled away from the others slightly. This will read as a grouping of three, or a *2 + 1* grouping, which is okay. Go figure!

Don't get too carried away with the odds

If you're inclined to work in odd numbers, be sure to mix up the numbers. A garden comprised solely of groupings of threes looks just as out of place as a garden comprised of groupings of fives or with no repetition of plants at all. Big-leaved, coarse-textured plants, such as cannas, have a large visual mass; so use a few of those and balance them with a greater number of fine-textured plants. Look at the sun plan again. The three cannas on the right are visually balanced by the surrounding number of smaller, fine-textured ornamental grasses and rushes.

So many plants, so little space

While odd numbers are generally preferred, limit the number of single specimens in your garden. While one of everything might be a good way to approach selecting gardening books for your library, it is often a visually chaotic way to approach plant selection. Having said that, we have colleagues and friends who may disagree. We joke that if you lined up carts at a garden center, you can tell who the designers are—we have multiples of a few plants, while the nondesigners have one of everything!

A background of evergreens sets the stage for deciduous shrubs & perennials

Plants with ornamental stems (redtwig dogwood, for example) can get lost if they don't have a good background to shine against. Likewise, small flowers or airy sprays of flowers show better against a dark background.

No mass of perennials should be big enough to leave a gaping hole in the winter

In the sun garden planting plan on page 71, bushclover, cannas, veronicas, and, most likely, iris (although some are evergreen) will be dormant in the winter. The roots will still be growing underground, but you'll only see a big area of mulch. However, notice how in the sun plan above, perennials are tucked in and around plants that are visible and add interest to the winter garden.

Something for every season

For best seasonal effect, design your rain garden with a mix of woody plants and perennials.

When selecting plants, think through what they offer in the different seasons. Flower color is outstanding, of course, but is often short-lived. A plant may have spectacular flowers for ten to fourteen days, but what about the rest of the year?

Some great solutions include the red chokeberry and American beautyberry—two fabulous shrubs that boast a variety of seasonal interest. The chokeberry has a multitude of white flowers in late spring/early summer and beautiful dark green foliage in summer. In fall, its color, a brilliant display of red and oranges, is unparalleled, and its red fruits attract birds. The beautyberry's summer flowers are small and not showy; its foliage is a lovely light green. However, come fall, the beautyberry boasts clusters of metallic magenta fruit with yellow foliage.

FIGURE 4-6
American beautyberry (right)
and red chokeberry (top)
have fruit that lasts into fall.

The habits of these plants are interesting in winter. The chokeberry has dark brown, fine-textured, upright branches; the beautyberry has buff-colored, coarser stems that arch gracefully. Year-round, these plants have pizzazz.

The key is to time periods of showiness, so there's always color in the garden.

FIGURE 4-7: A weeping river birch silhouetted against a sunny winter sky at the J.C. Raulston Arboretum in Raleigh, North Carolina.

Layering revisited

Many garden books advise you to layer plants, putting the shortest plants in the front of the bed and the taller ones in back. This is a fine approach. But when faced with so-called design rules, we try to think of reasons to break them!

FIGURE 4-8: Two views of a rain garden seen from all sides.

FIGURE 4-9: A large salvia planted in the front of this garden blocks the view of what is to come. It's unexpected. It's whimsical. It helps the garden look less formulaic.

If your garden will be viewed from more than one side, layer in the round, placing taller plants in the middle and shorter ones on the outside edge.

One of our favorite ways to rebel against design rules is to plant a large, lovely plant in the *front* of the bed (see Figure 4-9). The taller plant will obstruct views of the garden in its entirety, thus making the garden actually feel bigger than it really is and giving it a sense of expansiveness. Plus, when you have to explore a garden to see it all, it creates a sense of mystery.

Consider layering a large, fine-textured plant in front of a smaller, coarse one. You can see through the fluffiness of the plant in front to the more architectural one behind it (see Figure 4-10). That's great textural contrast! Combine that with fabulous color combinations as well, and your garden will be a visual feast.

GREAT PLANTS FOR RAIN GARDENS

Southern gardeners need to select plants based on the light and heat loads of their garden. With this in mind, we've grouped plants by light levels—shade, sun, and partial sun/shade. Within each of these general categories, plants are broken down by plant type—vines, ground covers, shrubs, and perennials.

Don't get us wrong. We *love* trees! It's just that the scale of most residential rain gardens isn't large enough for them. For gardeners working with larger sites, we've included a tree list at the end of this chapter.

The plants listed here have similar water requirements (belonging in a similar hydrozone) and will thrive in the South's hardiness and heat zones. They are *tough* ones—no frou-frou, fussy guys! They are pest- and disease-free, and low maintenance, not needing to be pruned regularly. And they're gorgeous plants that you should be able to find at local nurseries.

We list natives as well as non-natives, editing out some of our native plants that don't perform well in urban conditions, *and* including quite a few non-natives that are very well behaved! Also many cultivars of some species offer a variety of interest to the garden (for example, weeping forms of yaupon holly [*Ilex vomitoria*] and purple-leaved ninebarks [*Physocarpus opulifolius*]). And the species often offer different selections— e.g., flower colors, dwarf varieties, weeping forms—that grow well in rain gardens. A great example is the weeping bald cypress. It has a distinct, graceful weeping habit, but is small enough to fit into many gardens, attaining a height of ten to fifteen feet.

SHADE GARDEN

A shady garden site receives no direct sunlight and therefore is cooler than a sunny garden. In Figure 4-11 on the next page, the river birch leaves intercept most of the light, creating a cool growing environment beneath. Many shady gardens are also dry, so a rain garden is a welcome addition.

However, care must be taken when digging near trees not to damage roots. Tree roots radiate out from the trunk in all directions, extending two to three times the spread of the tree canopy. Because tree roots are found primarily in the top eighteen

FIGURE 4-10 (previous page): Looking through big bluestem.

FIGURE 4-11: Light that reaches this shade garden is filtered through the leaves of river birch trees.

inches of soil (where the most water and nutrients are), you'll encounter them when digging. Most trees can tolerate some root disturbance. But limit it to less than half the root system, not disturbing more than one side of the tree. The less disturbance, the better.

Shade gardens can be tricky; but when done properly, they're stunning. The plan on the following page uses three large evergreen shrubs as anchors—the medium-green, medium-texture Florida anise, the blue-green, medium coarse-texture leatherleaf mahonia, and the gray-blue, coarse dwarf palmetto. Contrasting the color as well as textures are two unique elderberry cultivars that round out the large shrub palette: The 'Black Lace' elderberry has dark purple foliage and pink flowers; the chartreuse, dissected-leaved elderberry adds *zing*.

Purple and chartreuse, or yellow, are one of our favorite color combinations, and in the shade garden this combination is repeated several times. A yellow acorus gathers next to the 'Black Lace' elderberry, while purple ajuga ground cover sits next to the

FIGURE 4-12: A planting plan for a rain garden in a shady location: A. white-berried nandina; B. Florida anise; C. 'Black Lace' elderberry; D. yellow acorus; E. sweetspire; F. epimedium; G. 'Illumination' vinca; H. cardinal-flower; I. Japanese aucuba; J. leatherleaf mahonia; K. Virginia bluebells; L. carex; M. cut-leafed yellow elderberry; N. inkberry; O. cinnamon fern; P. dwarf palmetto; Q. bugleweed.

yellow elderberry. Yellow is incorporated on the other side of the garden by using the 'Illumination' vinca.

This garden provides contrasts of colors (even different shades of green), textures, and habits. Take, for example, the coarse-textured, dark green-leaved Japanese aucuba paired with a large, variegated carex. These contrasting plants nestled together highlight *both* the carex and the aucuba, making them infinitely more interesting than using either one alone or without contrast.

Another key factor in this garden is the massing and layering of plants, giving the garden a natural look. Plants are grouped together and laid out in such a way as to *hug* one another (can't we all just get along?). No massing stops abruptly but flows softly into another, just as the joints in brick or stonework might be staggered to soften a transition.

Seasonally, the shade garden diagram has it all. In addition to the long-lasting foliage colors, bluebells provide electrifying color in the spring. Mahonia has showy bright yellow flowers in late winter/early spring. Sweetspire has white flowers in the summer. Cardinalflower also provides a brilliant red cluster in the summer. Epimedium (sometimes called fairy flower) has tiny yellow, pink, or purple flowers in the summer. In the fall the white, fruiting nandina backed by the darker green anise are gorgeous. The sweetspire and epimedium also put on glorious fall color displays.

FIGURE 4-13: A planting plan for a sunny rain garden: A. iris; B. Japanese spirea; C. dwarf nandina; D. mock-orange; E. winterberry; F. aster; G. maidenhair grass; H. American beautyberry; I. redtwig dogwood; J. dwarf yaupon holly; K. carex; L. canna; M. iris; N. yarrow; O. crocosmia; P. Kirilow indigo; Q. Japanese barberry.

FIGURE 4-14: Sun gardens receive direct sunlight at least six hours every day.

SUN GARDEN

A full sun garden receives direct sunlight for at least six hours a day. No relief here. Sun gardens are hot with high light intensity. Plants that can thrive in these conditions will definitely benefit from the extra water retained by the rain garden.

Seasonality is key in any garden. In addition to thinking about what looks good when, consider if certain plants actually look bad at times of year, and if so, what can be done about it.

In the sun garden plan (Figure 4-14), we'd like to draw your attention to two plants in particular: the American beautyberry and the redtwig dogwood. Both are known for their off-season interest—the beautyberry's purple fruit in the fall and the dogwood's redtwigs in the winter. The beautyberry has decent light green foliage in the summer and a lovely arching habit. The light pink flowers are small, but the metallic clusters of magenta fruits in fall are spectacular. However, after the fruit falls or is eaten by birds

FIGURE 4-15: Fall blooming asters are reliable color additions to a sun rain garden.

and before new spring foliage leafs out, the beautyberry is not at its best. It's best tucked in among other plants (evergreen and/or deciduous).

The same goes for the redtwig dogwood, albeit for slightly different reasons. This plant is famous for its vertical stems that turn bright red in winter (more pronounced in the northern regions of the Southeast). During the rest of the year, it's nothing to write home about: inconspicuous flowers, decent flat medium green, upright habit. In the summer, we use it simply as a background plant, biding our time, because the winter stem color is worth it.

Turning our attention to flowers, we need to get specific. Stretching out flowering times is important; simply saying, "summer blooming," doesn't quite cut it. To achieve continuous layering of color, you need to know when summer plants bloom and for approximately how long. Even within a plant species (e.g., *Iris* sp.), plants may bloom at different times. In the sun garden, we have plants blooming from late spring (the white-

FIGURE 4-16: A part-sun/part-shade garden receives only morning sun or filtered sun, and no hot afternoon sun that would damage these plants.

flowering mockorange and the pink-flowering indigo) to fall (maidenhair grass and aster).

Again, notice the overlapping plant masses in Figure 4-17—we can't stress this enough! Each mass looks fairly natural—at least avoiding *S* shapes! Each massing hugs the next one, so they relate visually. Single-file rows of plants in a naturalistic garden are a no-no. Abrupt changes feel . . . abrupt, like a visual hiccup.

PART-SUN/PART-SHADE GARDEN

A part-sun/part-shade garden either receives morning sun (none of that nasty, hot afternoon sun) or sunlight that filters through trees—making it cooler than a full sun site. The primary difference between a part-sun/part-shade garden and a shade garden is the intensity of sunlight—shade gardens have lower light intensity.

FIGURE 4-17: A planting plan for a rain garden in a part-sun/part-shade location: A. Florida anise; B. dwarf yaupon; C. bugleweed; D. fern; E. Siberian iris; F. fern; G. sweetshrub; H. southern wax myrtle; I. inkberry; J. summersweet clethra; K. sanguisorba; L. daylily; M. bellflower; N. hardy ageratum; O. dwarf fothergilla.

One thing all these designs share is a balance of evergreens, deciduous plants, and perennials. In the part-shade garden we want something showy every month of the year. Yes, we could do that easily with all evergreens, but that would be too easy, not to mention boring, as seasonal change would be greatly minimized or eliminated altogether.

When you analyze the plan in Figure 4-17, note two main design features: We plant an evergreen in close proximity to a deciduous shrub or mass of perennials to provide some color in the winter months. But we also use evergreens as backdrop plants. The purple/blue flowers of the hardy ageratum are lovely, but are more outstanding with the dark green holly behind them. The flowers of summersweet clethra are white or pink depending on the cultivar; and the fall color is a decent darker yellow. Beautiful on its own, it looks even more striking when backed by an evergreen.

"I understand your reasoning for combining evergreens and deciduous plants, but I am an evergreen plant freak!" you exclaim. "Can I achieve this effect with just evergreens?" Absolutely (if you must)! Imagine you are standing in the lower right of the part-shade garden. The layering of the anise, wax myrtle, and holly exhibits a subtle gradation of textures (larger leaves to smaller ones), and a variety of foliage colors (lighter green to olive green to dark green). Each plant is beautiful on its own, but when planted alongside plants of different textures, colors, and habits, it further enhances visual interest.

The second design feature involves the way the perennials are incorporated. When flowering and looking gorgeous, perennials are wonderful. Some go all summer, some for a much shorter period of time. When their show is over and they've gone dormant, you don't want a big area of nothing (*errr,* mulch!).

Anytime we incorporate a perennial mass (such as the bellflower, daylily, and iris), note that it's tucked between or next to shrubbery. The masses don't get too wide and tend to feather out at the ends. This ensures that when they go dormant, there's something in front of and/or behind to pick up the show-time slack. Other plants heretofore upstaged by the showy plants ensure that the garden remains beautiful, even though the perennials have retreated for the season.

Shade plants   D—DECIDUOUS; E—EVERGREEN; H—HERBACEOUS

NAME	TYPE	SIZE (h x w)	HABIT	FOLIAGE	OTHER NOTABLE FEATURES
Akebia quinata chocolate vine	D	20'–40'	Twining vine.	Bluish green foliage; medium texture.	Flowers not showy, but wonderfully fragrant in spring. Edible, chocolate-flavored fruit.

Shade ground covers   D—DECIDUOUS; E—EVERGREEN; H—HERBACEOUS

NAME	TYPE	SIZE (h x w)	HABIT	FOLIAGE	OTHER NOTABLE FEATURES
Ajuga reptans common bugle	E	3"–4"	Flat, mat forming.	Glossy green foliage; medium to coarse texture.	Many wonderful cultivars in variety of leaf colors in spring.
Liriope muscari liriope	E	18"–24" x 8"–12"	Upright.	Narrow, glass-like leaves; medium texture.	Dark purple spikes of flowers in summer. Green turning to shiny black fruit that persists through winter. Some variegated cultivars.
Liriope spicata creeping liriope	E	8"–12" x 6"–12"	Upright.	Very narrow leaves; fine texture.	Pale violet spikes of flowers in summer. Blue-black fruits. Many variegated cultivars. Can spread rapidly.
Vinca minor common periwinkle	E	4"–6"	Spreading dense mat.	Shiny dark green leaves; medium texture.	Small lilac-blue flowers in spring. Many variegated-leaved cultivars, even white-flowering ones.
Vinca major large periwinkle	E	8"–18"	Spreading dense mat.	Dark green leaves; medium texture.	Larger bright blue flowers than *V. minor* in spring. Also, variegated cultivar.

Shade shrubs   D—DECIDUOUS; E—EVERGREEN; H—HERBACEOUS

NAME	TYPE	SIZE (h x w)	HABIT	FOLIAGE	OTHER NOTABLE FEATURES
Aucuba japonica Japanese aucuba	E	6'–10' x 6'–10'	Upright.	Many cultivars with different leaf colors, some with variegated leaves; medium texture.	Red fruit persists through winter. 'Roxannie' fruits heavily. Tropical in appearance.
Calycanthus floridus sweetshrub or allspice	D	6' x 6'	Rounded.	Lustrous, dark green, deep vein patterns.	Deep red, fragrant flowers, not too showy; 'Athens' has chartreuse flowers; decent yellow fall color. Rapid spreading.
Ilex glabra inkberry	E	6' x 6'	Rounded.	Dark green; fine texture.	Dwarf cultivars available.
Illicium floridanum Florida anise	E	6'–8' x 5'–6'	Upright.	Dark green; medium texture.	Dark red flowers in late spring—not terribly showy.
Itea virginica Virginia sweetspire	D	6' x 4'	Upright, spreading.	Dull, medium green; medium-fine texture.	White summer flowers, excellent red fall color.
Mahonia bealei leatherleaf mahonia	E	4'– 8' x 4'–6'	Upright, rounded with age.	Deep green; coarse texture.	Yellow, fragrant flowers in late winter; bright blue fruit in summer.
Nandina domestica nandina	E	6'–8' x 2'–3'	Upright.	Bluish green, red in winter; medium texture.	White spring flowers, large clusters red-orange berries. Also white- and yellow-berried and dwarf cultivars.
Sabal minor dwarf palmetto	E	10' x 6'	Wide, yet upright.	Dark, bluish-green foliage; very coarse texture.	Hard to find in some areas. May look out of place if you don't have other tropical- looking plants.
Sambucus canadensis elderberry	D	6'–10' x 4'–8'	Leggy, open, arching.	Dull, light green; medium-fine texture.	White, flat-topped flower clusters in summer, purple fruit late summer. Attracts wildlife.

Shade perennials   D—DECIDUOUS; E—EVERGREEN; H—HERBACEOUS

NAME	TYPE	SIZE (h x w)	HABIT	FOLIAGE	BLOOM FORM, COLOR & TIME
Acorus spp. sweet flag	E	4"–8"	Stiff, upright, spreading.	Narrow, dark green; green with yellow, chartreuse foliage; strap-like; fine texture.	No flowers of consequence. Many species, cultivars. Chartreuse-foliage ones brighten shady garden, great when paired with coarse-texture plants!
Carex spp. sedge	E	8"–12"	Upright or slightly arching.	Strap-like foliage, green to white or yellow variegated; fine to medium-fine texture.	No flowers of consequence. Many species, cultivars in this genus—all great.
Chasmantheum latifolium northern sea oats	H	3' x 3'	Arching.	Loose, lance-like, gray-green; medium-fine texture.	Green fruit heads summer, turn bronze in fall.
Epimedium spp. epimedium	H	8"–10" x 18"	Spreading mound.	Triangular, dark green leaves (some mottled); medium texture.	White, pink, or yellow dainty flowers in late spring/early summer.
Iris cristata crested iris	H	3"–6"	Upright.	Strap-like, pale green foliage.	Blue flowers in spring.
Lobelia cardinalis cardinalflower	H	3'–5'	Upright.	Dark reddish purple; medium-fine texture.	Small, vertical clusters of red flowers in summer.
Lobelia siphilitica blue lobelia	H	1'–3'	Upright.	Narrow, strap-like; fine texture.	Small, vertical clusters of blue flowers in summer.
Mertensia virginica Virginia bluebells	H	1' x 1'	Low mound, with flowers standing above leaves.	Light green; medium-fine texture.	Small, light blue turning pink, funnel-shaped, early spring.
Osmunda cinnamonea cinnamon fern	H	2'–4' x 3'–4'	Graceful, upright, arching.	Light to medium green; medium-fine to fine texture; new fronds cinnamon color.	For foliage interest only.
Phlox divaricata woodland phlox	H	10"–20"	Upright.	Light green; fine texture.	Sky blue to violet in spring.
Polystichum acrostichoides Christmas fern	E	18"–36"	Arching.	Dark, but bright green; medium texture.	Foliage interest only.

Sun vines   D—DECIDUOUS; E—EVERGREEN; H—HERBACEOUS

NAME	TYPE	SIZE (h x w)	HABIT	FOLIAGE	OTHER NOTABLE FEATURES
Akebia quinata chocolate vine	D	20'–40'	Twining vine.	Bluish green foliage; medium texture.	Flowers not showy, but wonderfully fragrant in spring. Edible, chocolate-flavored fruit.
Gelsemium sempervirens Carolina jasmine	E	10'–20'	Twining vine.	Shiny green leaves; turns bronze in the winter; fine texture.	Yellow, fragrant flowers in spring.
Lonicera sempervirens trumpet honeysuckle	E – D	15'– 25'	Twining vine.	Medium texture.	Coral to red and yellow flowers midspring through fall, loved by hummingbirds. Many cultivars with different flower colors.

Sun ground covers   D—DECIDUOUS; E—EVERGREEN; H—HERBACEOUS

NAME	TYPE	SIZE (h x w)	HABIT	FOLIAGE	OTHER NOTABLE FEATURES
Liriope muscari liriope	E	18"–24" x 8"–12"	Upright.	Narrow, glass-like leaves; medium texture.	Dark purple spikes of flowers summer. Green turning shiny black fruit through winter. Some variegated cultivars.
Liriope spicata creeping liriope	E	8"–12" x 6"–12"	Upright.	Very narrow leaves; fine texture.	Pale violet spikes of flowers summer. Blue-black fruit. Nicely variegated cultivars. Can spread rapidly.
Vinca major large periwinkle	E	8"–18"	Spreading dense mat.	Dark green leaves; medium texture.	Larger bright blue flowers than *V. minor* in spring. Also, variegated cultivar.

Sun shrubs   D—DECIDUOUS; E—EVERGREEN; H—HERBACEOUS

NAME	TYPE	SIZE (h x w)	HABIT	FOLIAGE	OTHER NOTABLE FEATURES
Abelia x grandiflora glossy abelia	semi-E	3'-6' x 3'–6'	Spreading to rounded.	Glossy, dark green; medium texture.	White flower from early summer to frost. Some smaller and variegated-leaved cultivars.
Aronia arbutifolia red chokeberry	D	5'–6' x 3'–4'	Upright oval.	Glossy, dark green; medium texture.	White late spring/early summer flowers, showy red fruit in fall, orange/red fall color.
Berberis thunbergii Japanese barberry	D	3'–6' x 4'–7'	Rounded.	Medium texture.	Many cultivars in array of sizes, leaf colors.
Berberis julianae wintergreen barberry	E	4'–6' x 6'–8'	Rounded.	Olive green; medium texture.	Small yellow flowers in spring, bluish-black fruits persist through fall.
Buddleia davidii butterfly bush	D	5'–10' x 6'–8'	Rounded.	Gray-green to blue-green; medium to coarse texture.	Lavender, lilac, purple, white, yellow, or pink flowers in summer.
Callicarpa americana American beautyberry	D	4'–6' x 4'–6'	Open, loose, arching.	Medium green; medium texture.	Bright, vivid, purple fruit fall through early winter. 'Lactea' white fruit (good for evening garden). Small, inconspicuous flowers. Because of habit and winter interest, best tucked into garden.
Chaenomeles speciosa flowering quince	D	6'–10' x 6'–10'	Rounded.	Glossy green; medium texture.	Scarlet to red, pink, and white. Many cultivars with different flower colors.
Chionanthus virginicus, C. retusus fringetree, Chinese fringetree	D	12'–20' x 12'–20'	Rounded.	Pale green; medium texture.	Creamy-white, fragrant flowers in spring. Both species similar, but Chinese showier—flowers as leafing out, so flowers have built-in dark green background.
Cornus alba redtwig dogwood	D	3'–4' x 3'–4'	Very vertical, upright.	Flat green; medium texture.	Bright red stems in winter. White spring flower clusters nothing to write home about. Variegated foliage cultivar, 'Elegantissima'. Needs good circulation.
Hamemelis vernalis Ozark witch hazel	D	6'–10' x 6'–10'	Rounded.	Pale green; medium texture.	Strap-like red, yellow, or orange fragrant flowers late winter/early spring.
Hamamelis virginiana witch hazel	D	15'–30' x 15'–25'	Rounded.	Pale green; medium texture.	Delicately fragrant creamy to bright yellow flowers in fall.

NAME	TYPE	SIZE (h x w)	HABIT	FOLIAGE	OTHER NOTABLE FEATURES
Hibiscus syriacus shrub althea, rose of Sharon	D	8'–12' x 6'	Erect shrub or small tree.	Dark green; medium texture.	White to red, purple, or violet, or combination; single or double flowers summer through early fall. Many cultivars with different flower color.
Ilex cornuta 'Carissa' Carissa holly	E	3'–4' x 4'–6'	Rounded.	Yellow green; coarse texture.	Good background for lower-growing perennials.
Ilex glabra inkberry	E	6' x 6'	Rounded.	Dark green; fine texture.	Dwarf cultivars available.
Ilex verticillata deciduous holly, common winterberry	D	6' x 4'	Upright spreading.	Dull, medium green; medium texture.	Stellar orange or red fruit fall through winter (needs male and female plants for fruit production).
Ilex vomitoria yaupon holly	E	10'–15' x 8'–10'	Variable: upright, arching, or rounded and tight.	Dark green; fine texture.	Outstanding red fruit fall through winter. 'Pendula' beautiful weeping cultivar.
Indigofera amblyantha indigofera	D	4'–6' x 4'–6'	Rounded, loose.	Gray-green; fine texture.	Pale pink to rose, summer through fall.
Indigofera heterantha Himalayan indigo	D	4'–6' x 4'–6'	Rounded, loose.	Gray-green; fine texture.	Rose to purple in summer.
Indigofera kirilowii Kirilow indigo	D	2'–3' x 3'–4'	Densely upright.	Bright green; medium texture.	Pink in summer, makes good ground cover.
Magnolia stellata star magnolia	D	10'–20' x 10'–15'	Oval to rounded.	Light green; medium texture.	White, fragrant flowers in late winter/early spring.
Myrica cerifera Southern wax myrtle	E	10'–15' x 10'–15'	Upright rounded, spreading.	Olive green; medium texture.	Blue-gray fruit attracts many bird species.
Nandina domestica nandina	E	6'–8' x 2'–3'	Upright.	Bluish green, red in winter; medium texture.	White spring flowers, large clusters of red-orange berries. Also white- and yellow-berried and dwarf cultivars.
Philadelphus coronarius sweet mockorange	D	10'–12' x 8'–10'	Rounded.	Medium green; coarse texture.	White, fragrant flowers in spring.

NAME	TYPE	SIZE (h x w)	HABIT	FOLIAGE	OTHER NOTABLE FEATURES
Philadelphus inodorus, P. hirsutus scentless mockorange	D	6'–8' x 6'–8'	Loose, spreading.	Flat green; medium texture.	White flowers in spring.
Physocarpus opulifolius common ninebark	D	5'–10' x 5'–10'	Upright.	Flat green; medium texture.	Showy white or pink late spring/early summer flowers. 'Diablo' popular purple-leaved cultivar. 'Luteus' golden-leaved cultivar. Shaggy in winter, so tuck it somewhere.
Pyracantha koidzumii Formosa pyracantha	E	8'–12' x 8'–12'	Upright.	Flat green; medium texture.	Small white flowers in spring followed by red berries that persist into winter.
Sabal minor dwarf palmetto	E	10' x 6'	Wide, yet upright.	Dark, bluish-green foliage; very coarse texture.	Hard to find in some areas. May look out of place if you don't have other tropical plants.
Sambucus canadensis elderberry	D	6'–10' x 4'–8'	Leggy, open, arching.	Dull, light green; medium-fine texture.	White, flat-topped flower clusters in summer, purple fruit late summer. 'Laciniata Aurea'–cutleaf, chartreuse-leaved form. Attracts wildlife.
Sambucus nigra ' Eva' 'Black Lace' elderberry	D	6'–8' x 6'	Leggy, open.	Matte, purple foliage; fine texture.	Pinkish flat-topped flower clusters in summer.
Spiraea x bumalda Bumalda spirea	D	2'–3' x 3'–5'	Rounded.	Dark green; medium to fine texture.	White to pink flowers in summer.
Spiraea japonica Japanese spirea	D	2'–3' x 2'–3'	Mounded.	Light green or variegated; very fine texture.	Pink summer blooms. Many cultivars of different sizes and leaf colors. May seed.
Spiraea prunifolia bridalwreath spirea	D	4'–9' x 6'–8'	Upright, arching.	Blue-green leaves; medium to fine texture.	Double, button-like flowers in early spring.
Spiraea thunbergii Thunberg spirea	D	3'–5' x 3'–5'	Rounded.	Fine texture.	Small white flowers in early spring.
Spiraea x vanhouttei Vanhoutte spirea	D	6'–8' x 10'–12'	Vase-shaped.	Dark green; medium texture.	Many white flowers in spring cover most of stem.
Taxodium distichum 'Cascade Falls' Cascade Falls bald cypress	D	< 20' (possibly only 10'–12')	Weeping.	Bright, light green, ferny; fine texture.	Smaller, weeping version of common bald cypress. Leaves may turn bronze in fall.

NAME	TYPE	SIZE (h x w)	HABIT	FOLIAGE	OTHER NOTABLE FEATURES
Vaccinium corymbosum highbush blueberry	D	6' x 6'	Rounded.	Dull medium green; medium-fine texture.	White, late spring/early summer flowers; edible fruit midsummer. Good varicolored fall color.
Viburnum dentatum southern arrowwood	D	6' –10' x 6'–15'	Upright.	Dark green foliage turning yellow, crimson, purple fall color; medium texture.	Creamy white flowers in summer; blue to black berries through fall.
Viburnum lantana wayfaringtree viburnum	D	10'–15' x 10'–15'	Upright.	Dull blue-green; medium texture.	Creamy white flower. Yellow changing to red then black fruits in late summer.
Viburnum opulus European cranberry bush	D	8'–12' x 10'–15'	Upright, spreading.	Dark green; medium texture.	White flowers. Large clusters of bright red fruits from fall into winter.
Viburnum plicatum var. *tomentosum* Japanese snowball viburnum	D	8'–10' x 8'–10'	Tiered branching, rounded.	Dark green; medium texture; reddish purple fall color.	Large white flowers in spring cover most of branches. Bright red fruits turn black in summer.
Viburnum x pragense Prague viburnum	E	8'–10' x 8'–10'	Upright oval or oval rounded.	Lustrous dark green; medium texture.	Pink buds open into creamy white fragrant flowers.
Viburnum prunifolium blackhaw	D	12'–15' x 8'–12'	Upright.	Flat green changing to red- maroon in fall; fine texture.	Small white flowers clusters in spring. Yellow fruit turning bluish back in fall.
Yucca filamentosa Adam's needle yucca	E	2'–4'	Stiffly erect.	Sword-like leaves with sharp point; medium texture.	Creamy, white flowers on stalk 3'–4'. Several cultivars with gold leaves.

Sun perennials   D—DECIDUOUS; E—EVERGREEN; H—HERBACEOUS

NAME	TYPE	SIZE (h x w)	HABIT	FOLIAGE	BLOOM FORM, COLOR & TIME
Achillea millefolium common yarrow	H	1'–2'	Mounded.	Finely cut leaves; medium texture.	White to pink spring through fall.
Asclepias tuberosa butterfly milkweed	H	1'–3'	Upright.	Pale green; medium texture.	Orange-yellow to orange-red flowers in summer; loved by butterflies.

NAME	TYPE	SIZE (h x w)	HABIT	FOLIAGE	OTHER NOTABLE FEATURES
Aster spp. aster	H	1'–3'	Mounded.	Narrow leaves; fine texture.	Blue, purple, pink, or white flowers in fall.
Baptisia australis blue wild indigo	H	3'	Mounded.	Narrow leaves, gray-green color; fine texture.	Blue flowers in spring.
Calamagrostis acutiflora feather reed grass	H	4'–5' x 4'–5'	Vertical, tightly clustered.	Narrow, grassy, medium green; fine texture.	Bluish or pinkish panicle puffs in fall.
Canna spp. canna	H	3'–5'	Upright.	Bright, medium green (or multi-colored, dep. on cultivar); coarse texture.	Iris-like form; red, orange, yellow flowers in summer.
Carex spp. sedge	E	8"–12"	Upright or slightly arching.	Strap-like foliage, green to white or yellow variegated; fine to medium-fine texture.	No flowers of consequence. Many great species and cultivars.
Chasmantheum latifolium northern sea oats	H	3' x 3'	Arching.	Loose, lance-like, gray-green; medium-fine texture.	Green fruit heads in summer, turn bronze in fall; may seed in full sun.
Crocosmia spp. crocosmia	H	3'–4' x 3'–4'	Vertical.	Iris-like, medium green; medium texture.	Red, yellow, orange small flowers arrange linearly on stem midsummer.
Eupatorium coelestinum hardy ageratum	H	1'–3'	Rounded.	Pale green leaves; medium texture.	Small violet-blue flowers in clusters summer through fall. Spreads rapidly.
Eupatorium purpureum joe-pye weed	H	6' x 6'	Upright, spreading.	Dull, medium green; medium texture.	Pink/red flat-topped flower clusters late summer.
Gaillardia x grandiflora blanketflower	H	12"–36"	Mounded.	Dull green; medium texture.	Orange, yellow, red flowers all summer.
Helianthus spp. sunflower	H	5'–7'	Upright.	Medium texture.	Yellow flowers summer.

NAME	TYPE	SIZE (h x w)	HABIT	FOLIAGE	OTHER NOTABLE FEATURES
Heliopsis helianthoides heliopsis	H	4'–5'	Upright.	Medium texture.	Yellow to orange flowers summer.
Hemerocallis spp. daylily	H	foliage 1'–2', flower stalks up to 3 ½'	Arching.	Strap-like, linear; rich medium green; medium-fine to fine texture.	Funnel-shaped flowers in many colors; midsummer blooming.
Hibiscus coccineus rosemallow	H	6'–8'	Strongly upright.	Thread-leaf foliage; fine texture.	Large, bright red flowers summer.
Hibiscus moscheutos commoneyed rosemallow	H	4'–8' x 4'–8'	Loose, rounded.	Large, flat green, tropical-looking; coarse texture.	Enormous; white or many shades of pink. Blooms all summer.
Iris brevicaulis, I. fulva, I. hexagona, I. giganticaerula, I. nelsonii or any crossing of these Louisiana iris	H	2' x 2'	Upright.	Lance-like, darker gray-green; medium texture.	White, orange, yellow, purple, even maroon! Early summer.
Iris ensata Japanese iris	H	3' x 3'	Upright.	Lance-like, deep green; medium texture.	White, pink, lilac, blue in early summer.
Iris pseudacorus yellow flag	H	3' x 3'	Upright.	Lance-like, gray-green; medium texture.	Yellow, early summer. Rapid spreading.
Iris sibirica Siberian iris	H	3' x 3'	Upright.	Lance-like, deep green; medium texture.	Purple, late spring.
Iris tectorum Japanese roof iris	H	12"–18"	Upright.	Lance-like, deep green; medium texture.	Lilac flowers spring.
Iris versicolor harlequin blueflag	H	2' x 2'	Upright.	Lance-like, gray-green; medium texture.	Mostly purple with white splotch.
Juncus spp. rush	E	12"–36" x 12"	Upright.	Soft, tube-like stems, some twisted.	Greenish brown in summer.
Kniphofia uvaria redhot poker	H	1.5'–4'	Upright.	Lance-shaped leaves, not sharp; medium texture.	Red to orange to yellow flowers.

NAME	TYPE	SIZE (h x w)	HABIT	FOLIAGE	OTHER NOTABLE FEATURES
Lespedeza thunbergii bushclover	D	6' x 10'	Arching.	Blue-green; medium to medium-fine texture.	Showy, small but plentiful magenta pink flowers in summer; thrives on neglect, fast-growing.
Monarda didyma scarlet beebalm	H	2'–3' x 1'	Mounded.	Gray-green leaves; medium texture.	Red, white, pink, lavender in summer; attracts bees, butterflies, hummingbirds. Needs good circulation.
Muhlenbergia capillaris pink muhly grass	H	3' x 2'	Upright.	Dark green; fine texture.	Airy electric pink flowers; showy pink cloud late summer/early fall. Only ornamental grass to not look great in winter; cut back.
Panicum virgatum switchgrass	H	4'–6' x 3'	Upright.	Light green, blue-green; medium-fine to fine texture.	Loose red to purple panicles in late summer and fall.
Pennisetum alopecuroides fountaingrass	H	24"–36" x 24"–48"	Upright.	Light green, blue-green; medium-fine to fine texture.	Silver flowers in fall.
Penstemon digitalis smooth penstemon	H	2' x 2'	Upright.	Dark green; medium texture.	Small funnel, white. Blooms early summer.
Penstemon spp. beardtongue	H	18"–36" x 12"	Upright.	Deep green, some even reddish green; medium texture.	Bright pink, rose, white flowers. Blooms late spring.
Rudbeckia fulgida var. *sullivantii* 'Goldsturm' black-eyed Susan	H	18"–30" x 24"	Mounded.	Deep green; coarse texture.	Sunny yellow flowers with black center in summer. Will continue to bloom if deadheaded.
Salvia uliginosa sky-blue sage	H	48"–60" x 24"	Upright.	Blue-gray leaves; fine texture.	Sky-blue flowers in loose upright sprays in summer.
Schizacrium scoparium little bluestem	H	18" x 12"	Arching.	Light blue, gray, green foliage, often turns red and orange in fall; fine texture.	Slender silvery panicles, remain attractive through winter.
Solidago hybrids goldenrod	H	1'–3'	Rounded.	Pale green; medium texture.	Yellow flowers summer through fall.
Veronica noveboracensis ironweed	H	3'–6' x 3'–6'	Wild, shaggy.	Lance-like, medium green; medium-fine to fine texture.	Loose clusters of small purple, rose pink flowers late summer/early fall.

Veronica spicata spiked speedwell	H	12"–24" x 12"	Rounded, upright.	Dull, medium green; medium texture.	Spiky, purple/blue, mid- to late summer.

Part-sun/part-shade vines   D—DECIDUOUS; E—EVERGREEN; H—HERBACEOUS

NAME	TYPE	SIZE (h x w)	HABIT	FOLIAGE	OTHER NOTABLE FEATURES
Akebia quinata chocolate vine	D	20'–40'	Twining vine.	Bluish green foliage; medium texture.	Flowers not showy, but fragrant in spring. Edible, chocolate-flavored fruit.
Gelsemium sempervirens Carolina jasmine	E	10'–20'	Twining vine.	Shiny green leaves, turn bronze in the winter; fine texture.	Yellow, fragrant flowers in spring.
Lonicera sempervirens trumpet honeysuckle	E –D	15'–25'	Twining vine.	Medium texture.	Coral to red and yellow flowers midspring through fall; loved by hummingbirds. Many cultivars with different flower colors.

Part-sun/part-shade ground covers

D—DECIDUOUS; E—EVERGREEN; H—HERBACEOUS

NAME	TYPE	SIZE (h x w)	HABIT	FOLIAGE	OTHER NOTABLE FEATURES
Ajuga reptans common bugle capte	E	3"–4"	Flat, mat forming.	Glossy green foliage; medium to coarse texture.	Many wonderful cultivars in variety of leaf colors in spring.
Liriope muscari liriope	E	18"–24" x 8"–12"	Upright.	Narrow, glass-like leaves; medium texture.	Dark purple spikes of flowers in summer. Green turning shiny black fruit persists through the winter. Some variegated cultivars.
Liriope spicata creeping liriope	E	8"–12" x 6"–12"	Upright.	Very narrow leaves; fine texture.	Pale violet spikes of flowers in summer. Blue-black fruits. Many variegated cultivars. Can spread rapidly.
Vinca minor common periwinkle	E	4"–6"	Spreading dense mat.	Shiny dark green leaves; medium texture.	Small lilac-blue flowers in spring. Many variegated-leaved cultivars, even white-flowering ones.
Vinca major large periwinkle	E	8"–18"	Spreading dense mat.	Dark green leaves; medium texture.	Larger bright blue flowers than *V. minor* in spring. Also, variegated cultivar.

Part-sun/part-shade shrubs   D—DECIDUOUS; E—EVERGREEN; H—HERBACEOUS

NAME	TYPE	SIZE (h x w)	HABIT	FOLIAGE	OTHER NOTABLE FEATURES
Agarista populifolia (Leucothoe axillaris) Florida leucothoe	E	8'–12' x 6'–8'	Arching.	Glossy green; medium texture.	Fragrant white flowers in spring, can be heavily pruned to keep smaller.
Aronia arbutifolia red chokeberry	D	5'–6' x 3'–4'	Upright oval.	Glossy, dark green; medium texture.	White late spring/early summer flowers; showy red fruit in fall; orange/red fall color.
Aucuba japonica Japanese aucuba	E	6'–10' x 6'–10'	Upright.	Many cultivars with different leaf colors, some with variegated leaves; medium texture.	Red fruit persists through winter; 'Roxannie' fruits heavily; tropical-looking.
Berberis thunbergii Japanese barberry	D	3'–6' x 4'–7'	Rounded.	Medium texture.	Many cultivars in array of sizes and leaf colors.
Callicarpa americana American beautyberry	D	4'–6' x 4'–6'	Open, loose, arching.	Medium green; medium texture.	Bright, vivid, persistent purple fruit fall through early winter. 'Lactea'—white fruit (good for evening garden). Because of habit and lack of winter interest, best tucked into garden. Small, inconspicuous flowers.
Calycanthus floridus sweetshrub or allspice	D	6' x 6'	Rounded.	Lustrous, dark green; deep venation; medium to medium-coarse texture.	Deep red, fragrant flowers, not showy; 'Athens'—chartreuse flowers; decent yellow fall color. Rapid spreading.
Chaenomeles speciosa flowering quince	D	6'–10' x 6'–10'	Rounded.	Glossy green; medium texture.	Scarlet to red, pink, and white. Many cultivars with different flower colors.
Chionanthus virginicus, C. retusus fringetree, Chinese fringetree	D	12'–20' x 12'–20'	Rounded.	Pale green; medium texture.	Creamy-white, incredibly fragrant flowers in spring. Species similar, except Chinese showier (flowers same time as leafs out)
Clethra alnifolia summersweet clethra	D	6' x 3'	Upright oval.	Glossy medium green; medium texture.	White summer flowers, yellow fall color.
Fothergilla gardeni dwarf fotherfilla	D	5' x 5'	Rounded.	Dull, blue-green leaves; medium texture.	White mini-bottlebrush type flowers in spring; red/orange fall color.

NAME	TYPE	SIZE (h x w)	HABIT	FOLIAGE	OTHER NOTABLE FEATURES
Hamemelis vernalis Ozark witch hazel	D	6'–10' x 6'–10'	Rounded.	Pale green; medium texture.	Strap-like red, yellow, or orange fragrant flowers in late winter/early spring.
Hamamelis virginiana witch hazel	D	15'–30' x 15'–25'	Rounded.	Pale green; medium texture.	Delicately fragrant creamy to bright yellow flowers in fall.
Ilex glabra inkberry	E	6' x 6'	Rounded.	Dark green; fine texture.	Dwarf cultivars available.
Ilex vomitoria yaupon holly	E	10'–15' x 8'–10'	Variable—upright, arching, or rounded and tight.	Dark green; fine texture.	Outstanding red fruit fall through winter; 'Pendula'– beautiful weeping cultivar.
Itea virginica Virgina sweetspire	D	6' x 4'	Upright, spreading.	Dull, medium green; medium-fine texture.	White summer flowers; excellent red fall color.
Mahonia bealei leatherleaf mahonia	E	4'–8' x 4'–6'	Upright, rounded with age.	Deep green; coarse texture.	Yellow, fragrant flowers in the late winter; bright blue fruit in summer.
Myrica cerifera southern wax myrtle	E	10'–15' x 10'–15'	Upright rounded, spreading.	Olive green; medium texture.	Blue-gray fruit attracts multitude bird species.
Nandina domestica nandina	E	6'–8' x 2'–3'	Upright.	Bluish green, red in winter; medium texture.	White spring flowers, large clusters red-orange berries. Also white- and yellow-berried and dwarf cultivars.
Philadelphus coronarius sweet mockorange	D	10'–12' x 8'–10'	Rounded.	Medium green; coarse texture.	White, fragrant flowers in spring.
Philadelphus inodorus (P. hirsutus) mockorange	D	6'–8' x 6'–8'	Loose, spreading.	Flat green; medium texture.	Nonfragrant white flowers in spring.
Sabal minor dwarf palmetto	E	10' x 6'	Wide, yet upright.	Dark, bluish-green foliage; very coarse texture.	Hard to find in some areas. May look out of place if you don't have other tropical plants.
Sambucus canadensis elderberry	D	6'–10' x 4'–8'	Leggy, open, arching.	Dull, light green; medium-fine texture.	White, flat-topped flower clusters in summer, purple fruit late summer. S. nigra 'Eva', 'Black Lace' elderberry— purple foliage, pink flowers. Attracts wildlife.

NAME	TYPE	SIZE (h x w)	HABIT	FOLIAGE	OTHER NOTABLE FEATURES
Taxodium distichum 'Cascade Falls' Cascade Falls bald cypress	E	< 20' (possibly only 10'–12')	Weeping.	Bright, light green, ferny; fine texture.	Smaller, weeping version common bald cypress! Leaves may turn bronze in fall.
Viburnum dentatum southern arrowwood	D	6'–10' x 6'–15'	Upright.	Dark green foliage turning yellow, crimson, purple fall color; medium texture.	Creamy white flowers in summer; blue to black berries through fall.
Viburnum lantana wayfaringtree viburnum	D	10'–15' x 10'–15'	Upright.	Dull blue-green; medium texture.	Creamy white flower. Yellow changing to red then black fruits in late summer.
Viburnum nudum possumhaw	D	12' x 9'	Upright, spreading.	Dark blue-green; medium texture.	White, flat-topped flower clusters in midsummer, blue fruit in fall, red to purple fall color. Attracts wildlife.
Viburnum opulus European cranberry-bush viburnum	D	8'–12' x 10'–15'	Upright, spreading.	Dark green; medium texture.	White flowers. Large clusters of bright red fruits in fall that persist into winter.
Viburnum plicatum var. *tomentosum* Japanese snowball viburnum	D	8'–10' x 8'–10'	Tiered branching, rounded.	Dark green; medium texture; reddish purple fall color.	Large white flowers in spring cover most branches. Bright red fruits turn black in summer.
Viburnum x pragense Prague viburnum	E	8'–10' x 8'–10'	Upright oval or oval rounded.	Lustrous dark green; medium texture.	Pink buds open into creamy white fragrant flowers.
Viburnum prunifolium blackhaw	D	12'–15' x 8'–12'	Upright.	Flat green changing to red-maroon in fall; fine texture.	Small white flowers in clusters in spring; yellow fruit turns bluish back in fall.

Part-sun/part-shade perennials

D—DECIDUOUS; E—EVERGREEN; H—HERBACEOUS

NAME	TYPE	SIZE (h x w)	HABIT	FOLIAGE	BLOOM FORM, COLOR & TIME
Baptisia australis Blue wild indigo	H	3'	Mounded.	Narrow leaves, gray-green color; fine texture.	Blue flowers in spring.
Campanula americana tall bellflower	H	36"	Upright.	Fine texture; a great see-through plant.	Violet-blue summer through fall; self-sowing.

NAME	TYPE	SIZE (h x w)	HABIT	FOLIAGE	OTHER NOTABLE FEATURES
Carex spp. sedges	E	8"–12"	Upright or slightly arching.	Strap-like foliage, green to white or yellow variegated; fine to medium-fine texture.	No flowers of consequence. Many great species and cultivars.
Eupatorium coelestinum blue mistflower	H	1'–3'	Rounded.	Pale green leaves; medium texture.	Small violet-blue flowers in clusters summer through fall.
Iris cristata crested iris	H	3"–6"	Upright.	Strap-like, pale green foliage	Blue flowers in spring.
Iris brevicaulis, I. fulva, I. hexagona, I. giganticaerulea, I. nelsonii, or any crossing of these Louisiana iris	H	2' x 2'	Upright.	Lance-like, darker gray-green; medium texture.	White, orange, yellow, purple, even maroon, early summer.
Iris ensata Japanese iris	H	3' x 3'	Upright.	Lance-like, deep green; medium texture.	White, pink, lilac, blue in early summer.
Iris pseudacorus yellow flag	H	3' x 3'	Upright.	Lance-like, gray-green; medium texture.	Yellow, early summer. Rapid spreading.
Iris sibirica Siberian iris	H	3' x 3'	Upright.	Lance-like, deep green; medium texture.	Purple, late spring.
Iris tectorum Japanese roof iris	H	12"–18"	Upright.	Lance-like, deep green; medium texture.	Lilac flowers in spring.
Juncus spp. rush	E	12"–36" x 12"	Upright.	Soft, tube-like stems, some twisted.	Greenish brown in summer.
Lobelia cardinalis cardinalflower	H	3'–5'	Upright.	Dark reddish/purple; medium-fine texture.	Small, vertical clusters of red flowers in summer.
Lobelia siphilitica blue lobelia	H	1'–3'	Upright.	Narrow, strap-like; fine texture.	Small, vertical clusters of blue flowers in summer.

NAME	TYPE	SIZE (h x w)	HABIT	FOLIAGE	OTHER NOTABLE FEATURES
Miscanthus spp. maidenhair grass	H	18"–8' x 15"–5'	Upright, gently arching.	Medium green, or green with white, or green with yellow dep. on cultivar; medium-fine to fine textured.	Gorgeous foliage accent—even when dormant in winter. Many cultivars of different heights and foliage colors.
Monarda didyma Scarlet beebalm	H	2'–3' x 1'	Mounded.	Gray-green leaves; medium texture.	Red, white, pink, lavender in summer; attracts butterflies, bees, hummingbirds. Needs good circulation in partial shade to prevent/reduce mildew (or use facer plant to hide foliage).
Phlox divaricata woodland phlox	H	10"–20"	Upright.	Light green; fine texture.	Sky blue to violet in spring.

SAMPLE TREE LIST

Some trees listed here may be too big for most rain gardens. But they're excellent choices for residential sites. Some also filter pollutants. All will survive both wet and dry conditions.

Black alder (*Alnus glutinosa*)

Black locust (*Robinia pseudoacacia*)

Common bald cypress (*Taxodium distichum*)

Dawn redwood (*Metasequoia glyptostroboides*)

Japanese flowering apricot (*Prunus mume*)

Juneberry/serviceberry (*Amelanchier laevis* or *A. arborea*)

Pawpaw (*Asimina triloba*)

Poplar (*Populus* spp.)

Red buckeye (*Aesculus pavia*)

River birch (*Betula nigra*)

Sweetbay magnolia (*Magnolia virginiana*)

FIGURE 4-18: Sometimes fall can surprise you with the most amazing color combinations—in this case *Cotinus coggyria* (smokebush) and *Amsonia montana* 'Short Stack'.

PLANT BUYING 101

When you've plotted out a general design and put together a plant list for your rain garden, the next step is to purchase plants. Look for plants with healthy leaves (no holes, good color) and good shape.

Size of the plant doesn't matter. Big plants and small ones will thrive. The most important part of the plant to carefully consider is the root. Before you buy, pull the plant out of the pot, if possible. The roots should fill the pot and hold the planting media together in a firm root ball.

DIG IN

Now it's time to plant those perfectly purchased plants correctly. Many gardeners have a tendency to plant either too shallowly or too deeply. The depth of the hole should be an inch shallower than the depth of your plant's root ball, so that the surface of the media in which the plant is growing is about an inch above the soil surface.

Dig a hole slightly wider than the plant's root ball in your beautifully amended filter bed. Because a tangled mass of circling roots will be slow to grow into the surrounding soil, you'll want to loosen the root ball so the roots will easily grow out into the soil. To loosen the root mass from the media, knock it against a hard surface and then use your fingers to loosen the spiraled roots.

Or, take a knife and make three to four slashes, cutting the roots in the root ball to a depth of about an inch. This will not hurt the plant's roots but will instead encourage them to grow into the soil.

After you've put the plant into the hole, fill soil in around the loosened root ball. Then cover the area with mulch.

RAIN GARDEN MAINTENANCE

We hate to break the news to you, but every garden needs *some* maintenance. Fortunately, rain gardens require no more maintenance than do traditional gardens. In fact, because they don't need as much irrigation, they may require less work.

First, let's look at irrigation. Unless it rains frequently (every three to five days in the summer, every five to seven days in the fall), a newly planted rain garden will need to be watered until the plants' roots are established in the filter bed. (Fall is a great time for planting because the plants require a lot less irrigation.)

It takes three to six months for perennials to become established and six to twelve months for trees or shrubs. Once established, the rain garden will need to be irrigated only during an extended drought.

Rain garden plants will also need some fertilizer. Just how much depends on the amount of nutrients the garden receives in the runoff from the rest of the landscape. Runoff usually contains some nutrients that can be used by the plants, which is the whole point of a rain garden—to capture these nutrients before they pollute our waters. Therefore, it's essential to perform a soil test that will determine the nutrient levels in the rain garden's filter bed. Applying fertilizer where it's not needed defeats the whole purpose, killing your garden's plants and contributing to water pollution.

Any fertilizer applied to the rain garden should be a slow-release formulation of the nutrients needed. Many fertilizers are very water-soluble and, in a rain garden's moisture-rich soil, might filter down into underground water reserves. Coated slow-release fertilizers, composts, or slowly soluble formulations of fertilizers are good choices.

The winter months are the best time to prune and cut back many perennials and shrubs. By removing the dead above-ground growth of most herbaceous perennials in the winter, you make room for new growth in the spring.

Another bit of maintenance is deadheading—removing dead flowers. If you do this in the spring and summer, you may encourage reblooming and eliminate any unwanted spreading by seed.

Shrubs that flower in the summer should also be pruned during the winter to remove unwanted growth and maintain the health and appearance of the shrub. Shrubs that flower in the spring should be pruned after they flower.

Because there is less plant growth to damage, winter is also a great time to mulch. Depending on how fast the mulch in your rain garden decomposes, you should apply two inches of mulch to your garden about every two to three years. Mulch will prevent weed growth and erosion as runoff moves into the rain garden.

MOVING ON

Perhaps by now you have designed and installed your rain garden. How exciting! We hope the plants are thriving. The rain garden should be capturing, holding, and filtering runoff correctly, as well as minimizing the amount of runoff leaving your property. With any luck the rain garden is also providing you much enjoyment.

Sometimes things don't work out quite as planned, however, and you may run into some gardening snafus. The next chapter, "Troubleshooting," should answer most of the questions or address the problems you might be experiencing (well, with your rain garden, anyway! There's not much we can do to help you with the dog that mistakes your prized banana shrub for a fire hydrant!).

CHAPTER 5

TROUBLESHOOTING

Let's start with the good news: Not a lot can go wrong with a rain garden. After all, you've chosen a good garden site, prepared a wonderful soil environment in the filter bed, chosen plants that adapt well to the garden environment, and planted them correctly.

Even when you've done everything right, things can still go wrong. Gardens are complex ecosystems with a lot of factors that affect plant survival. Below are some common mishaps and our suggestions of possible ways to overcome them.

Poor drainage—water still standing three days after a rain

Rainfall needs to drain quickly from the rain garden to prevent plant death and mosquito breeding. If you find water still standing in the rain garden three days after a rainfall, here are some things to consider:

- Examine the filter bed's drainage. The soil may not have enough large pores to allow the water to drain well. If you have not yet planted the plants, work more amendment into the soil in the filter bed. Make sure the amendment you choose has large enough particles—some at least as large as a half inch in length. Pine bark or compost work well for this situation.

-

- If the garden already has been planted, you can dig the amendment into areas around the plants, working it into the soil at least six inches deep.

- The berm may be too tall. If so, it could be trapping the water, causing the rain garden to capture more water than it can drain. To solve this problem, lower the berm so that it doesn't trap as much water. Or, make the rain garden bigger to enable it to absorb more water.

- Soil may have washed into the rain garden covering the mulch. Fine-textured soil will drastically slow water moving into the filter bed. To alleviate this problem, scrape out the soil that washed in and reapply the mulch.

- The soil in the filter bed may have become compacted. This can be caused by either natural settling or from walking too much in the garden during planting and maintenance. Loosen the soil with a digging fork. Work more amendments into the filter bed's soil. Reapply mulch. To avoid compacting the soil, do not walk in the rain garden when the soil is very moist.

Drainage too fast; established plants dying

A newly planted rain garden requires irrigation until the plants have become established. When the plants' roots have grown into the soil of the filter bed, plants should be able to survive on just the water captured by rainfall. If well cared for in that critical developmental stage, herbaceous flowering plants can usually thrive on their own after three months and woody trees or shrubs after six months. If established plants in your rain garden are dying, consider the following:

- The filter bed may not be holding enough water to meet the plants' needs. To remedy this, work some small-particle-size (less than a half inch in length) amendment into the filter bed. Because compost has a wide variety of particle sizes—large and small—it also works well as an amendment in this situation. Dig the amendment into the soil at least six inches deep around the plants throughout the garden. Apply more mulch, which will reduce the amount of water that evaporates out of the soil. Select a mulch that has both large and small particles to help trap water.

- Also, consider making the berm taller so that the garden traps more water during rainfall events.

- Has it rained recently? Is the soil dry? Apply irrigation, preferably using drip irrigation, to supplement the garden's water needs. Soaker hoses are an easy and inexpensive way to provide drip irrigation to a garden and can be connected to a rain barrel to utilize water saved from a rainy day!

- If your dying plants are covered with pests (bugs or diseases), get in touch with your local agricultural extension office for help diagnosing and treating pest problems.

New plants dying

While they acclimate to their new environment, newly planted garden plants must be kept moist. This allows their roots to spread and become strong enough to learn how to deal with water stress. If newly planted plants are dying, consider the following issues:

- You may not be watering often enough or deep enough. A plant needs about an inch of water a week to establish itself successfully. This water needs to be applied directly to the soil around the plant.

- Plastic gallon milk jugs are an efficient way to apply this water. Poke a small hole in the bottom of the jug. Place it next to the plant. Fill the jug with water. The water will slowly ooze out, irrigating with no runoff! To lessen the not-so-beautiful aesthetics of a bunch of milk jugs in your garden, you can paint the jugs earth colors or get and wild and crazy with the color choice! Plants are usually established within three months for herbaceous perennials and within six months for woody shrubs and trees.

- Make sure the plants are healthy to begin with. Purchase plants from a reputable nursery or garden center. Carefully inspect the plants before you buy to make sure there are no holes in the leaves, and that they're bug- and disease-free, and nicely shaped. Pull the plants out of the pots and inspect the roots to best determine the plants' health. The roots should be growing out to the edges of the pot and be firm, not slimy or with white tips. The planting media should smell organic, not sour.

- Also make sure the plants were planted correctly. If planted too shallowly or too deeply, plants will die. The surface of the media in which the plant grows should be approximately an inch above the soil surface. Plants take in oxygen and give off other gases where the branches or trunk join the roots (called the crown). Mulch should then be applied over the exposed roots in the root ball, but the mulch should be pulled back from the stem of the plant.

Mulch washing out; erosion occurring

When water moves quickly across the soil surface, mulch washes with it. To prevent mulch from washing out of the rain garden, you must take steps to slow the speed at which water enters and moves through the garden. One, or a combination, of these techniques should work:

- Use a heavier mulch with larger particles or different-sized particles that can nest together.

- Do not let runoff enter the rain garden from a single point. Spread the flow of runoff, and thus its impact, into the rain garden over as wide an area as possible.

- Place some rocks where runoff enters the rain garden to slow it.

- Where the runoff enters the garden, plant ground cover or plants with many branches that originate from the soil's surface, such as ornamental grasses, carex, or sedges. The stems of the plants will slow runoff and encourage it to enter the rain garden's filter bed.

Mushroom invasion!

Mushrooms are fungi and don't damage plants. Saprophytic creatures that feed on decaying organic matter, mushrooms love moist places that are rich in compost, like the rain garden. Mushrooms are actually good guys that add humus to soil. But there are some important things to consider:

- Some mushrooms are poisonous if ingested. Mushroom identification is as much an art as it is a science, and therefore is best left to the pros. If you have pets or small children that might be tempted to taste them, scoop the mushrooms up with a shovel and add them to your compost pile.

- Some fungi are nasty looking. One of our favorite ugly guys is called dog vomit fungus—you can imagine what it looks like. Dog vomit fungus grows on top of organic mulches after a good rainfall. It is not poisonous, but can spread throughout the garden and may even spread across low-growing plants. Like other unwanted fungi, it should be removed because it can shade-out and kill some shorter plants.

EXTENSION SERVICE CONTACTS IN THE SOUTH

We've tried to anticipate typical problems to troubleshoot. But nature has ways of forever surprising us. If you have a rain garden problem that isn't addressed in this chapter, you have various resources at your disposal; but one of the best is your local land-grant state university agricultural extension service.

Every land grant university has three missions—teaching, research, and extension. (At least that's presently the case; loss of federal funding is threatening their existence.) Extension, the outreach arm of these universities, is charged with sharing unbiased, researched-based information with the citizens of the state.

Below is a list of the land grant universities in southern states. Local extension offices are usually listed in the government pages of your local phone book. Homepages for extension programs have also been listed. There you'll often find local extension office contact information for each county in the state.

Alabama

LAND GRANT UNIVERSITIES

Alabama A&M University

Auburn University

Tuskegee University

ALABAMA COOPERATIVE EXTENSION SYSTEM

http://www.aces.edu/

Georgia

LAND GRANT UNIVERSITIES

Fort Valley State University

University of Georgia

UNIVERSITY OF GEORGIA COOPERATIVE EXTENSION

http://www.caes.uga.edu/extension/

FORT VALLEY STATE UNIVERSITY COOPERATIVE EXTENSION PROGRAM

http://www.fvsu.edu/about/external-affairs/cooperative-extension

North Carolina

LAND GRANT UNIVERSITIES

North Carolina A&T State University

North Carolina State University

NC COOPERATIVE EXTENSION SERVICE

http://www.ces.ncsu.edu/

South Carolina

LAND GRANT UNIVERSITIES

Clemson University

South Carolina State University

CLEMSON UNIVERSITY COOPERATIVE EXTENSION
http://www.clemson.edu/extension/

1890 EXTENSION PROGRAM
http://www.scsu.edu/1890/extension.aspx

Virginia

LAND GRANT UNIVERSITIES

Virginia Polytechnic Institute and State University

Virginia State University

VIRGINIA COOPERATIVE EXTENSION
http://www.ext.vt.edu/

It's worth becoming familiar with your state land grant university's website. You'll find a wealth of information there. You also can look up your local extension office by name, discipline, institution, position, or email from the website below:

- https://people.extension.org/colleagues (registration required)

Or you can search by state and then by county using this website:

- http://www.csrees.usda.gov/Extension/

CHAPTER 6

OTHER WATER-WISE GARDENING OPTIONS

We love rain gardens and hope one day soon to see them thriving in yards every-where. However, you may want to consider other water-wise gardening practices that can be used with or without a rain garden. For example, rain harvesting (using rain barrels and/or cisterns) prevents runoff by capturing and storing rainwater that you can then save and use on a non-rainy day. Minimizing impervious surfaces when possible is also a good practice, and new building materials offer some attractive alternatives to asphalt and traditional concrete surfaces.

These practices may be especially viable for locations that have runoff issues but aren't suitable for a rain garden. Maybe you have a downspout that deposits water into an isolated area where it cannot be directed away from your home's foundation. Maybe you have a garden that cannot be converted to a rain garden; and harvested rain can be stored and used, as needed, to water that garden.

Rain chains, rain barrels, cisterns, drip irrigation, and porous concrete are some of the ways home gardeners are minimizing runoff and maximizing rainwater to use in their landscapes. In this chapter, we explore the possibilities.

FIGURE 6-1

A rain chain directs roof runoff into a buried drainage pipe that flows into the rain garden at the North Carolina Wildlife Commission building, North Carolina State University.

RAIN BARRELS

Capturing rainwater is as old as the hills. Across America, after years of burying drainpipes and letting our rainwater mysteriously disappear into sewer systems, we're rediscovering the ancient technique of rain harvesting.

The devastating drought that much of the South experienced in 2007 has made the rain barrel a gardening staple. There's nothing like scarcity to make us appreciate a precious resource we long took for granted. And, given the amount of rain that flows down our gutters, even during a light rain, rain harvesting is becoming a gardening requisite. (See "Rain barrel size" opposite.)

Rain barrel shoppers have many options—tall, stout, big, small, black, white, even faux terra cotta. At its most basic, a rain barrel is a container that holds water, can withstand freezing winter temperatures, and can be sealed off to prevent mosquito breeding. Thin-walled plastic containers, such as large trash cans, may be okay for a short-term solution during warm weather. But they usually crack during the expansion and contraction caused by water freezing and thawing during winter months.

Likewise, rain barrels also need to be made of a material that will not break down in sunlight.

The color of the rain barrel is also important. A rain barrel needs to be a dark color to prevent sunlight from penetrating and supporting algae growth. Many large barrels are white. If white is the only color available, you can paint the rain barrel with a dark, outdoor paint that adheres to plastic. If your house is yellow or another light color and you don't want a big black rain barrel sticking out like a sore thumb, you can cover the black paint with a paint color to match your house.

Rain barrel aesthetics

Most rain barrels are not terribly attractive. But with a little creativity, you can make them disappear.

Some homeowners place them near air conditioning units and then hide both behind fencing or shrubs. Vines can be grown on the fence or on a trellis to make it blend into the landscape. A screen of evergreen shrubs or vines will also shade the barrel, preventing algae growth.

If you have a raised deck, it may be possible to put the rain barrel underneath, and hide it that way.

Regardless of where you put the barrel and what you put around it, be sure to leave sufficient access around the rain barrel (and the air conditioner), so that you'll be able to harvest the water.

Rain barrel size

Choosing the most appropriate rain barrel size is a difficult decision for the home gardener. Considerations include volume—how much rain you'll capture—as well as the footprint of the rain barrel.

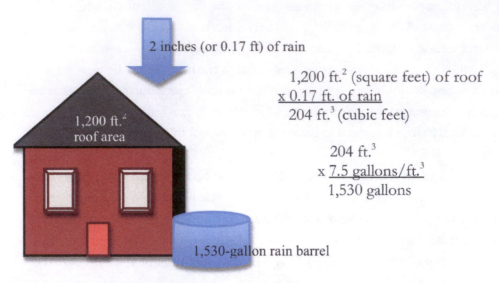

2 inches (or 0.17 ft) of rain

1,200 ft.² roof area

1,200 ft.² (square feet) of roof
x 0.17 ft. of rain
204 ft.³ (cubic feet)

204 ft.³
x 7.5 gallons/ft.³
1,530 gallons

1,530-gallon rain barrel

FIGURE 6-2: Calculating ideal rain barrel size.

Getting a barrel large enough to capture a substantial amount of runoff is paramount. A one-inch rain falling on 1,000 square feet of roof generates 625 gallons of water. And this is just *one* one-inch rain. Additional rainfall will cause a rain barrel that's only big enough to capture those first 625 gallons to overflow, causing soggy soil and erosion around the barrel. If the rain barrel is located near the home's foundation, overflow can be a real problem.

To calculate the size of the rain barrel you need, calculate the surface area of roof (*length* x *width*) from which you want to capture runoff. Multiply this area by the amount of rainfall you want to be able to capture and contain. (A good estimate is the weekly rainfall during the spring months.) Multiply the roof area by the rainfall amount, and then multiply that total by 7.5 (one cubic foot of water equals 7.5 gallons) to convert this to gallons of water.

Most rain barrels sold on the market are too small. A 50-gallon rain barrel cannot capture much runoff. A 0.25-inch rain falling on only 26 square feet of roof yields 50 gallons of water. While you can connect several 50-gallon rain barrels together by using their overflow pipes, you have to purchase and deal with the footprint (and aesthetics) of a row of rain barrels. Ultimately, it may be more cost-effective and more attractive to simply purchase a large rain barrel.

FIGURE 6-3
A whiskey barrel and copper rain chain fit into the design of this informal landscape.

FIGURE 6-4
Gutters empty into a large rain barrel. Notice the overflow pipe that directs excess water into a nearby rain garden.

FIGURE 6-5
A faucet and hose are used to water thirsty plants in the garden.

After you've calculated the volume of the rain barrel you want, you then need to decide on the footprint, the amount of ground space the barrel will require. Measure the space before you purchase the barrel to ensure it will fit. Rain barrels can be tall and narrow or short and wide. Large rain barrels are frequently six feet or larger in diameter.

Installation

Most rain barrels come with a faucet installed near the bottom. If yours doesn't, it's relatively easy to install one. Make sure you install a faucet made of frost-proof material that won't crack in the winter.

There's nothing more frustrating than having a barrel full of water and not being able to get much or any of it to come out of the hose hooked up to the barrel's faucet. To improve water pressure, raise the rain barrel to increase the gravitational pull. You

FIGURE 6-6: Two different styles of rain chains in action.

can use bricks, stones, or concrete blocks, any material that will be stable and strong enough to hold a full barrel of water.

When you have the rain barrel level and painted, you need to direct water into the barrel. You can insert a gutter directly into the barrel, use a flexible gutter connector, or use a rain chain, from which water will flow down into the barrel. Regardless of how the water gets there, it's critical that the barrel not be left uncovered.

In Figure 6-3, window screen is attached to the top of the rain barrel with a piece of wire. The overflow is positioned two inches below the lip of the barrel so that when the water level reaches that point (just below the screen), it will flow out the overflow valve into the ground. (See "A full barrel" on the next page.) Thus, mosquitoes cannot reach the water. They're crafty critters and will lay eggs through the screen if the screen is in contact with the water.

FIGURE 6-7: Large decorative rain barrels at the North Carolina Aquarium on Roanoke Island.

A full barrel

If you capture a week's rainfall during the rainy season, you'll have a nice reserve of water. But at that time of year, odds are you'll have more rain before you have a chance to use any of the stored water.

Therefore, it's important to have an overflow valve that directs the water away from the house. If there isn't one on your rain barrel, it's a good idea to install one connected to a pipe that can direct excess water to a place where you want it, ideally toward a rain garden or other landscape plantings.

Cisterns

The difference between a rain barrel and a cistern basically comes down to two factors: size and location. Cisterns are larger than rain barrels (often with more than 10,000 gallons in capacity) and are frequently buried in the ground.

FIGURE 6-8

A 300-gallon rain barrel is hidden behind
foundation shrubs. Two downspouts from
the gutter direct runoff into the rain barrel.

THE WATER-WISE DRIP IRRIGATION

Drip-irrigation systems are the most water-efficient method of irrigating a garden.
They also can be hooked to a faucet or rain barrel.

Drip irrigation need not be fancy or elaborate. Soaker hoses are excellent for slowly
irrigating a garden that is level. (Because soaker hoses are not pressure compensated,
they shouldn't be used to irrigate sloping garden spaces.)

If not hooked into a public water source, a drip-irrigation system can be easily
designed around it. With every foot drop in elevation, 0.433 psi (pounds per square

FIGURE 6-9: Flexible poly pipe is connected to a ball valve (controls the water flow) and a union (used to disconnect drip irrigation system from the rain barrel during winter) on the rain barrel. The poly pipe can withstand winter temperatures and can be hidden under mulch. Middle, a filter in the poly line removes any debris that has collected in the rain barrel. Here, a screen filter provides an inexpensive, easy way to clean water. A union lets the filter be easily removed and stored during winter. Right, a network of in-line drip irrigation branches from the flexible poly pipe delivering water to the garden.

inch) of pressure is gained. With a garden planted on a slope, the natural drop in elevation may generate enough water pressure to operate a drip-irrigation system.

Most drip-irrigation systems require very little water pressure, and therefore can be hooked up to a rain barrel, which also can be raised on a platform to increase water pressure. Figure 6-9 shows a series of images illustrating how you can construct a drip-irrigation system using a rain barrel.

POROUS HARDSCAPES

Driveways and patio areas are welcome additions to many home landscapes. These functional spaces need not create runoff problems because of their impervious surfaces. Consider instead using a material on your driveway like porous concrete, which allows

FIGURE 6-10: Porous concrete and non-mortared bricks make water-wise, environmentally favorable hardscapes.

FIGURE 6-11: Left, the turf paver is exposed in a high-traffic area; right, drains are used to remove standing water from walkways.

water to infiltrate its surface. Bricks or other pavers, set in a bed of sand, also let water soak into the ground and make very attractive patios.

Gravel and turf also can be used to create stable, permeable surfaces for parking and walkways. In Figure 6-11, a drain is installed to remove runoff from a low area in a gravel walkway. The runoff is diverted into a nearby garden space. Turf pavers are rigid plastic supporters that can be covered with either gravel or turf to create a stable surface for a patio or temporary parking area.

A SOIL PRIMER

Most people garden because they love plants, flowering or otherwise. Some may want to grow food for their family. Others just love being outside. However, early in every gardener's education, she or he realizes that soil is the key to success. Sure you have to buy healthy plants, site them properly in the landscape, and plant them correctly. But unless the soil is good, success is unlikely.

We remember when we were second-year horticulture students being required to take a class called, Introduction to Soil Science. *Soil is a science?* we wondered. *When did that happen?* Even after our first class, we still had doubts about the need to learn about different types and properties of soil. Boy, were we wrong.

Soil is more than just dirt, more than just rocks. Soil is a combination of small pieces of mineral rocks and organic matter in various states of decay. It's a dynamic ecosystem, teeming with life that interacts with a plant's roots, aiding the plant in its quest for water, nutrients, and oxygen—all three of which are needed by the roots of plants. Without any one of those, the roots will die—and to quote a dear friend, "No rootie, no shootie."

Fortunately, one does not have to learn every member and its role in a soil ecosystem to understand how the system works. Basically soil has five components: parent material, pore space (air-filled and water-filled), organic matter, nutrients and pH, and microbes including earthworms.

Parent material is the rock from which soil is formed. The rock's mineral composition, along with the topography and climate of an area, time, and the soil microbes, determines the soil's ability to supply water, nutrient, and oxygen.

The soils in most of the Southeast are old, weathered by many years of high temperatures and rainfall.

Clay is the largest mineral component in most of our region's soils. Clay particles are flat and stack together closely, creating long, thin gaps (called pores) between the particles. These small, thin pores hold water tightly enough that gravity cannot pull the water down toward groundwater supplies quickly. Thus it takes seven to ten days for a wet clayey soil to drain. As water drains from the pores, it is replaced by air.

A clayey soil needs to be irrigated with an inch of water only once a week. However, because clayey soils do not have large pores, water cannot move (infiltrate) into the soils quickly; so irrigation is best applied by a drip-irrigation system. Also, clay's slow infiltration rate makes it unsuitable for a rain garden's filter bed unless it's amended.

Isolated areas of the Southeast have soils with large fractions of sand, a larger particle than clay. Sand, which is a round particle, doesn't nest together as well as clay. Sand leaves larger gaps (pores) between the particles. Gravity can more easily pull water from these larger, more rounded pores, meaning that sandy soils are well aerated and drain in two to three days.

Because infiltration is rapid in sandy soils, sprinkler irrigation is appropriate. However, it requires less water more often: Only a quarter inch of water should be applied four times a week. Sandy soils don't hold water well so they're also not appropriate for a rain garden's filter bed unless they're amended.

Now let's look at organic matter. Excluding isolated pockets of the Southeast where alluvial deposits (soils carried to an area by a river or stream) of organic matter have formed highly organic soils, most soils in this region are low in organic matter. (Home landscapes where the topsoil has been removed during construction are lacking in organic matter.) Organic matter glues soil particles together into clumps (called aggregates), creating a complex system of small and larger pores that holds water and drains at different rates. This mixture of pore sizes means that a more even supply of both air and water are present to support root growth.

A soil with a good mix of mineral particles and organic matter will crumble easily and is referred to as being friable. When you crumble a handful of rich, friable soil, you can imagine how easily a plant's roots could push their way through and get everything they need—water, nutrients, and air. (Earthworms and soil microbes also thrive in a friable soil.)

Organic matter is most easily and affordably added to soil in the form of compost. Any compost is good compost, although different compost has different levels of

FIGURE A-1: Left, moist ball of soil; center, making a ribbon; left, ribbon less than a half-inch long.

nutrients—composted manures having much higher levels of nutrients than composted yard waste. All organic matter must be composted (allowed to break down and decay) before it can be mixed into the soil as an amendment. But organic materials, except manures (which must be composted), do not require composting before being used as a mulch.

DETERMINING YOUR SOIL'S TEXTURE

It's pretty easy to figure out what kind of soil you have in your garden. Take a small handful of it and add enough water so that you can mold it into a ball. Press the soil gently between your thumb and forefinger, trying to stretch out a ribbon.

If the soil is sandy, you may have difficulty making a ribbon. If you can make a ribbon, the next step is to notice the feel of the soil as you're working it: Is it gritty or sticky? Based on the length of the ribbon you form and the feel of the soil, you should be able to use the table below to determine your soil type.

Sand	Will not form a ribbon of any length and has a nonsticky, grainy feel.
Sandy loam	Will form a ribbon less than a half inch in length and feels gritty.
Clay loam	Will form a ribbon less than an inch in length and feels smooth and only slightly sticky.
Clay	Will form a ribbon longer than an inch in length and feels smooth and sticky.

When it comes to the success of your rain garden, the only difference between the soils in the table above is their infiltration rates and ability to hold water (drain slowly).

However, none of these soils makes for a perfect filter bed alone. All benefit from soil amendments. Though not very romantic, soil amendments are the best investment of time and money a gardener can make.

Soil amendments are determined by the desired goal for the soil. Clayey soils need large particles added to increase large pores spaces. Pea gravel, tire mulch, aged pine bark, and compost are all great amendments for such soils.

Sand should never be added to clayey soils. *Sand + clay + heat = bricks*—not good for growing conditions. Sandy soils need amendments that will increase the number of small pores, which will help the soil hold water better. Such amendments include aged pine bark and compost. Peat moss can be used, but it's a natural resource that's being depleted; so it's best to choose another material.

Hardwood bark, sawdust, and wood chips are not good soils amendments for any soil. They continue to decompose in the soil and remove nitrogen that plants need.

Now let's think about rain falling on loose, beautifully amended soil. As a raindrop falls on the soil, it enters a large pore (infiltration). When that large pore fills with water, it overflows into the next smaller pore, and so on, until most of the pores in the upper regions of the soil are full of water.

After a rain, water in these pores moves laterally, filling all the smaller pores, and then moves downward as gravity pulls the water from the larger pores. Plant roots intercept and drink up the water from all sizes of pores except the very, very small pores, which hold water so tightly that the roots cannot break it free. Unfair isn't it! Your poor plant will be wilted and parched, surrounded by water in the soil that it can't drink.

Eventually, the water will be pulled down by gravity, below the level at which the plant's roots can reach it. Roots can only grow as deep as oxygen moves into a soil. The myth that there are deep-rooted and shallow-rooted plants is just that—not based in reality! Plant roots grow where there is water, nutrients, and oxygen.

If the soil lacks enough large pores to allow oxygen to move into it, the roots will grow only at the surface where they can get oxygen. The better a soil is amended and the larger the mixture of pores, the deeper roots will grow, because the plant will have greater volume of soil to exploit for water, nutrients, and oxygen. Thus the need for a well-developed filter bed.

Still water will be pulled downward toward deep-water reserves—which is where we want it to end up. However, once water seeps below where plant roots can grow, it's lost to the plant, as are any nutrients (e.g., nitrogen and phosphorus) that have dissolved in it.

Other aspects of soils (nutrients, pH, soil microbes, and earthworms) are interconnected. Of these, the soil pH determines the success of the rest.

The combination of parent material and the period of long weathering has left many soils with high iron levels (hence the red color) and low pH levels. At low pH levels, plant roots cannot take nutrients from the soil. Most garden plants need soil pH at a level between five and six.

To determine how to adjust a garden's pH, have your soil tested by a professional soil-testing laboratory. Attempting to guess and apply liming products without a test may have disastrous consequences. (Contact your local extension office to find out how to submit a soil sample. See Chapter Five, "Troubleshooting," for information on finding your nearest Extension office.)

The starting point for any successful garden is analyzing your soil and adjusting it appropriately, based on the results from the professional soil analysis. Additionally, good soil microbes and earthworms flourish in soil with an appropriate pH. Nice how that works!

After you get to know your soil, gardening is easy and fun—plants flourish, pest problems are reduced. All you have to do is sit back and enjoy!

ADDITIONAL RESOURCES

Environmental Protection Agency (EPA)

http://cfpub.epa.gov/npdes/stormwatermonth.cfm

http://cfpub.epa.gov/npdes/home.cfm?program_id=6

The Rain Garden Network

http://www.raingardennetwork.com/

Rain Gardens: A how-to manual for homeowners

http://clean-water.uwex.edu/pubs/pdf/home.rgmanual.pdf

North Carolina Extension Service Backyard Rain Gardens

http://www.bae.ncsu.edu/topic/raingarden/

Plant Facts

http://www.ces.ncsu.edu/depts/hort/consumer/factsheets/

KEY TERMS & CONCEPTS

BERM: A raised area that can direct water flow into, as well as retain, water in the rain garden.

DRAINAGE: The rate (inches per hour) at which water moves down through the soil below plant roots and toward groundwater supplies.

FIGURE G-1: Measuring drainage.

How to measure drainage:

Dig a hole six inches deep.

Fill the hole with water.

If the soil is very dry and the water drains from the hole quickly, fill the hole again.

Wait one hour.

Using a ruler, measure how far down the water drained out of the hole.

This is the soil's drainage rate in inches per hour.

DRIP IRRIGATION: Water is applied very slowly to the soil in a garden by either small drippers or small holes in the irrigation pipe. Drip irrigation doesn't waste as much water as sprinklers, because water is applied directly to the soil where roots are growing. Therefore, water doesn't evaporate or become runoff, because it's applied slowly enough that it matches the soil's infiltration rate.

FIGURE G-2: Measuring infiltration.

INFILTRATION: The rate (inches per hour) at which water moves into soil.

How to measure infiltration:

Remove the top and bottom or a soup can and push can one inch into the soil.

Carefully insert a coffee can, also with the top and bottom removed, over the soup can into the soil one inch deep with space around the soup can. (Do not rock the soup can as you push.)

Fill the coffee and soup cans with water, till both are filled to the top of the soup can.

Wait thirty minutes. Fill both again. Wait thirty more minutes.

Using a ruler, measure how far the water level has dropped in the soup can.

Multiply this amount by two. This will give you the inches/hour rate, which is the soil's infiltration rate.

MULCH: Spread over the surface of a garden to decrease water evaporation and weed growth.

FIGURE G-3: The plant on the left is planted too deeply. The plant on the right is correctly planted.

PLANTING: For a garden plant to grow successfully, it must be planted correctly—the root ball must be loosened and planted at the correct depth.

FIGURE G-4: A well-amended soil has a mixture of particle sizes and organic matter blended evenly throughout the growing bed.

RUNOFF: Rain or irrigation water that is not absorbed into the soil. It then runs into storm water systems, carrying with it pollutants such as soil, nutrients, and organic matter.

SOIL AMENDMENT: A substance mixed into soil to change the soil's infiltration and drainage properties. Soil amendments can be organic (e.g., compost, shredded leaves, pine bark) or inorganic (e.g., gravel, PermaTill). Amendment choice depends on drainage, infiltration, and the native soil's texture (sandy or clayey), although organic amendments also increase organic matter in soil.

STORM WATER COLLECTION SYSTEM: Runoff, water that flows across the earth's surface, is directed into a storm drain, covered with a grate. The grate prevents large pieces of debris from entering the underground pipes that carry the runoff to a water treatment plant. However, small debris and other pollutants are carried in the runoff, eventually being released directly into a lake or stream or being directed to public wastewater treatment systems.

SWALE: A depressed area that can direct water flow into a rain garden.

TRANSPIRATION: The loss of water as vapor from the leaves of a plant.

BIOGRAPHIES

Helen Kraus holds BS, MS, and Ph.D. degrees in Horticultural Science from North Carolina State University, where she currently teaches. Her research interests include best management practices, including irrigation management and compost utilization for the containerized plant production nursery industry. Dr. Kraus teaches a variety of classes including Nursery Management and Tree and Grounds Management; but her favorite teaching subject is Principles of Horticulture, which includes an introduction to plant growth and environmental influence on plant growth as well as environmentally responsible gardening practices.

Anne Spafford holds a BS degree in Ornamental Horticulture and an MLA in Landscape Architecture from the University of Illinois. She teaches in the Department of Horticultural Sciences at North Carolina State University. Her classes range from introductory landscape design, site design and construction materials, a landscape construction studio, as well as planting design and residential landscape design—all based on sustainable and envirornmentally friendly landscape practices.

INDEX

CPSIA information can be obtained
at www.ICGtesting.com
Printed in the USA
BVHW021325120323
659789BV00002B/32